The
Garland Library
of
War and Peace

The
Garland Library
of
War and Peace

Under the General Editorship of
Blanche Wiesen Cook, *John Jay College, C.U.N.Y.*
Sandi E. Cooper, *Richmond College, C.U.N.Y.*
Charles Chatfield, *Wittenberg University*

The Essays
of Philanthropos on
Peace and War

by
William Ladd

with a new introduction
for the Garland Edition by
Peter Brock

Garland Publishing, Inc., New York & London
1971

Library of Congress Cataloging in Publication Data

Ladd, William, 1778-1841.
    The essays of Philanthropos on peace and war.

    (The Garland library of war and peace)
    1. Peace--Addresses, essays, lectures. 2. War--
Addresses, essays, lectures. I. Title. II. Series.
JX1949.L18 1972   327'.172   76-147434
ISBN 0-8240-0221-0

Printed in the United States of America

Introduction

During the War of 1812, a New England sea captain named William Ladd (1778-1841) had retired from the merchant navy as a result of the dislocation of trade caused by hostilities and had settled on his family farm at Minot in Maine. Ladd liked country pursuits, and the avocation of gentleman farmer left him plenty of leisure to devote to the various causes in which he was interested. Fat and jovial, he does not appear at first sight to have been the kind of person whom we might expect to find leading a moral crusade, even if an early concern for the antislavery movement showed that he was indeed a reformer by inclination. Yet the "American peace crusade" (as Merle E. Curti has called the antebellum peace movement) owed more to Ladd, perhaps, than to any other single person. He was in charge of the American Peace Society's activities for the first decade after its foundation in 1828, acting as secretary of the Society. Eventually he came to accept the full pacifist position; however, his influence was always on the side of moderation, of reasonable compromise so long as basic principles were not repudiated. As secretary of the A.P.S. he continued the policy of Noah Worcester, who had been responsible in 1815 for setting up the first peace society in New England, and accepted into membership all who wished sincerely to work for peace. "Not William Penn himself", writes Ladd's successor as secretary of the A.P.S., George C. Beckwith, "was more thorough on peace, yet [Ladd] . . . did not expect men to come, at a single leap, the whole length of any reform." A sensible, kindly and tolerant man, who was both practical and at the same time genuinely idealistic and sincerely religious, he is one of the most attractive figures in the history of the early American peace movement. True, his ecumenical spirit proved unable to prevent the split which occurred in the late 1830's when the radical nonresistants broke off from the A.P.S. to form their own peace organization. Yet he remained on good terms with the dissidents and, until his death, continued to exert his utmost to heal the breach.

Peace was a latecomer among the reform causes to which Ladd gave his enthusiastic support. But in the end antislavery, home and foreign missions, Sunday schools, temperance, and the welfare of seamen and of the American Indians were all to take second place for him behind the overriding demands of the peace movement. Henceforward it was to the cause of peace that he devoted most of his time and energy: his fluent pen and his eloquent tongue were equally at the movement's disposal.

The publications of the Massachusetts Peace Society, including Worcester's famous tract, A Solemn Review of the Custom of War *(1814),* had *first aroused Ladd's interest in the cause of peace. He joined his local peace society and began to contribute articles on the subject of peace and war to the* Christian Mirror, *"a religious newspaper, printed at Portland, Maine." It was these articles that in 1827 he collected and published anonymously as the* Essays of Philanthropos on Peace and War. *Curti has called these essays "incisive, practical, and realistic in their arguments." They might surely gain the assent of both a Quaker absolutist and a supporter of defensive wars, though it is clear that Ladd already entertained strong doubts concerning the compatibility of war with the Christian religion as well as the possibility of defensive warfare ever occurring if Christians lived up to the principles of their faith. In successive essays Ladd unmasks the sordid motives, which lie behind practically all international conflicts, and reveals the immorality, brutality and waste, which appear to be inseparable from war and preparation for war. Finally, he appeals to "the female sex", to ministers of religion, and to Christians in general (whose master is "the Prince of Peace") to use their influence to counteract the baneful attraction that in the past "the custom of war" has exerted on mankind.*

True, there is little that seems original to us today in what Ladd has to say. But it needed courage and independence of mind to speak out in his day against war. The peace advocates of that period, if they were not mocked and scorned, were usually ignored. Ladd wrote in the original preface to these essays: "The present edition is small. If the book should take, a larger edition may be printed. If it should not, let it die. But ... it may do good. If it does, I am satisfied." Ladd's satisfaction if he could have known that his little volume would be reprinted almost a century and a half after its first publication would undoubtedly have paled, however, before his realization that "the promised empire of PEACE", to which he looked forward eagerly at the conclusion of this same preface, still appears to be as remote a vision today as it seemed to be in his own time.

Peter Brock
Department of History
University of Toronto

THE ESSAYS

OF

PHILANTHROPOS

ON

PEACE & WAR,

Which first appeared in the Christian Mirror, printed at
Portland, Maine.

REVISED AND CORRECTED

BY THE AUTHOR.

SECOND EDITION.

"On earth Peace, and Good will to Men."

EXETER, N. H.

PUBLISHED BY JOHN T. BURNHAM, IN BEHALF OF THE
EXETER, AND OTHER PEACE SOCIETIES, AND SOLD BY
F. GRANT, EXETER; J. B. MOORE, CONCORD; M. NEW-
MAN, ANDOVER; J.W. FOSTER, PORTSMOUTH; W.HYDE,
PORTLAND; C. WHIPPLE, NEWBURYPORT; WHIPPLE
AND LAWRENCE, SALEM; LINCOLN AND EDMANDS,
BOSTON; COOK AND SONS, AND ANDREWS, HARTFORD;
H. HOWE, NEW-HAVEN; J. LEAVITT, AND J. P. HAVEN,
NEW-YORK; CAREY AND LEA, PHILADELPHIA; R.BOYL-
STON, AMHERST; J. PRENTISS, KEENE; HOLBROOK
AND FESSENDEN, BRATTLEBOROUGH.

1827.

PREFACE.

—◆—

I FEEL no diffidence, nor timidity in presenting the following Essays, (which have already appeared in the Christian Mirror, a religious newspaper, printed at Portland, Maine) to the public, in a new form. I neither court nor deprecate criticism. It is sufficient for me, that some, whose opinions I value very highly, have thought that they *have been* productive of good, and that, by a more extended circulation, they *may be* productive of more.

It is true that the anti-christian spirit, the deleterious nature and the demoralizing and destructive consequences of WAR have been laid before the American public, by the Friend of Peace, by a few tracts, published by the Peace Societies of New-York and Philadelphia, by occasional addresses, and by a few,

—very few sermons. Yet it is certain, that thousands of our fellow citizens have never had an opportunity of reading a single page on the subject of *permanent and universal peace,*—that there are thousands of others, who have so wrapped themselves up in impenetrable prejudice, as to be scarcely tangible by any means. And with sorrow I am compelled to add, that there are many devout and benevolent christians,—as much averse from war as I am—as much convinced of its sinful nature and horrid consequences, both temporal and eternal,—who yet fold their arms in listless apathy, and do not move a finger, to promote a cause, for which they daily pray, and neglect even to put the weight of their example into the scale of Peace. I was formerly as indifferent as they, but by reading the "Friend of Peace," casually lent me by a friend, I perceived that it was my duty, to watch as well as pray. Many of my neighbors, who were prejudiced against the cause, have become advocates for Peace; and many

in various parts of America and Europe, have
been very much excited, in the good cause;
and so far as this spirit extends, so far the
empire of Peace is established.

In republishing these essays, I have made
but few alterations. Titles have been added
to each number. A few typographical errors
have been corrected. A few passages have
been made plainer, and a few notes have been
added. I am sensible, that many inelegan-
cies remain—but it is not worth the trouble
to correct them—for, though the rounding
of the periods may raise the *author*, in the
estimation of some, the *subject* would gain
but little if any advantage. Perspicuity and
brevity have been my object; and perhaps
I have, sometimes, sacrificed one to the other;
—it will only require a little more attention
in the reader. In fine, I am willing that the
critics—if they think me worthy of their notice—should find as much fault as they please
with my *style*, if they will only acknowledge
the correctness of my *conclusions*.

1*

The present edition is small. If the book should take, a larger edition may be printed. If it should not, let it die. But as nothing is more capricious than public opinion, it *may* do good. If it does, I am satisfied.

That God would be graciously pleased to bless my labors and make them instrumental of hastening the promised empire of PEACE, when nation shall no more lift up sword against nation, nor learn war any more, is the fervent prayer of the Public's already much obliged and humble servant,

PHILANTHROPOS.

NO. 1.

Introduction.

In consequence of reading the "Friend of Peace," and other tracts published by the Massachusetts Peace Society, which were given me by a friend, I became convinced that war is an evil, which might be banished from civilized society, and that it is the duty of every man to lend a helping hand to bring about so desirable an event. I felt it a duty, which I owe to God and to my fellow-creatures, to do something to hasten the glorious era, when men shall learn war no more: which certainly will come as predicted in the Holy Scriptures, but which, like the conversion of the world, must be brought about by God's blessing on the exertions of the benevolent. Every individual is responsible for his conduct in this respect. He who does not give his prayers, his influence, his talents, and, if necessary, his purse to hasten the Millennium, fails in his duty as a christian and a man. Under these impressions, I became a member of the Peace Society of Maine, and received about twenty numbers of the tracts published by the Massachusetts Peace Society. Those I had before received from a friend I got bound into a volume, to lend among my neighbors. I have been anxious-

ly inquiring for the remaining numbers, that
I might bind the others also, and send them
on a like errand.   But all my inquiries have
been fruitless.   I have understood that there
have been one or two anniversaries of the
Peace Society of Maine celebrated at Portland ; but, on inquiry, could never learn the
day of the year on which the anniversary
occurred, nor the names of the officers.   It
seems that while smarting under the evils of
our last war, and shocked by the accounts
of bloodshed, havoc and misery, which were
brought by every arrival from Europe, Christians and philanthropists thought that something must be done.   But when war was
suspended and peace restored to the wearied
nations, and no signs of war remained among
christian states except some struggles for
liberty, they seemed to think the purpose accomplished, and to have relaxed their exertions ; forgetting that the same causes will
always produce the same effects ; and that
the evil of war will not cease, until there
shall have been a radical change in the opinion of mankind respecting it.   When the
opinion of one individual is changed, something is done towards the great result.   But
continued and unremitted exertions of the
friends of peace are necessary, and perhaps
will be necessary for one or two centuries,
before the grand event will be fully accomplished.   But that it will be accomplished,
we are certain ; and that it will be by means
of peace societies, in connexion with the ex-

tension of the christian religion, is probable. In the mean time, their exertions will
not be without their reward ; wars will become less frequent, and less cruel. An evident change in public opinion has been already effected.

I wish, Sir,* that you or some of your
correspondents would give us some account
of the Peace Society of Maine ; the names
of its officers, the day of its anniversary, its
means, &c. Also of the Massachusetts Peace
Society ; how many tracts they have published, and how they may be obtained. It
seems the more necessary that something
should be done, as the flame of war is again
lighted in Europe, and how far the conflagra-
tion will extend we know not. " The beginning of strife is as when one letteth out
water." A small leak in a dyke soon occasions the destruction of the whole, and the
deluging of the adjacent country. Who
would have imagined the desolating wars occasioned by the French revolution ? The
Spanish revolution may occasion as many ;
and as we were involved in the other, so may
we be in this.†

---

* As these essays were at first addressed to the editor of
the Mirror, I did not think it worth while to alter the
phraseology.

† In consequence of this and some of the succeeding
numbers, the Peace Society of Maine celebrated their anniversary with an address and appropriate exercises, and
has since been reorganized and become more efficient than
ever.

NO. 2.

Changes in Public Opinion.

I SENT you some inquiries concerning the Peace Society of Maine; but my mind is so full of the subject that, without waiting for an answer to that communication—which I hope to see in due time, either from yourself or some of your numerous correspondents, I sit down again to trouble you with some of my thoughts on *universal peace*;—I hope, however, the subject will soon be taken out of my hands, by some able writer in your interesting paper; for I consider it proper for investigation in the Christian Mirror, as ultimately connected with the eternal interests of mankind.

I think we have no reason to be discouraged from attempting something in this way; for, independently of the hopes set before us in the gospel, the history of mankind shows us such great changes in public opinion, that we need not despair. I say *public opinion;* for the continuance of war rests *entirely* on that. Let every person do what he can to effect this change, and the work is done. We look back with wonder and astonishment at the delusions of ancient times, in the same manner as future generations will look on the fatal delusions of a spirit of war; and the present generation has witnessed changes in public opinion, which a century ago would have been deemed incredible.

Not to go beyond the christian era for ora-
cles, omens, and augurs, which have passed
off with gods of wood and stone, let us contemplate the astonishing delusions of nominal christians, and the abominable practices
founded on them, which have been removed
by a change in public opinion. What do we
think now of the ordeal of the burning
plough-share, the hot iron ball, hot and cold
water, &c. practised as late as the twelfth
century? What do we think of the trial by
battle, which has continued in some degree
to our own days, but which has fallen into
contempt with all men of a just sense of
honor, and is reserved for the exclusive use
of Cummings, McDuffie, and Co? Had any
one, 700 years ago, while the ploughshares
were heating or the lists preparing, predicted
that the time would come, when these *holy*
trials would be held in just detestation, and
give place to trials by jury; he would have
appeared less worthy of credit than the man
who should now predict that in a few centuries the practice of war will be looked upon
with a like detestation, and disputes between
states and empires be settled by amicable adjustment or arbitration.

Where is now the power of the " man of
sin," with his relics, his indulgences, his in-
fallibility, and his inquisition? They are all
fallen together. Their only support was
public opinion, and that has changed. Who
would have thought, 314 years ago, when
Luther commenced the reformation, that so

great a change would be by this time effected,—a change as great, as far as it extends,
which is to the whole christian name—as any
we anticipate? If so great a change has
been wrought by the instrumentality of one
man, what encouragement is it for us to
press forward.

But not to confine our remarks to popery,
we must observe that protestantism also has
had her " acts of faith," her stake and fagot,
and popery in turn her martyrs. But who
now thinks of correcting a man's faith by
burning his body?

Nor is the *name* of religion to bear all the
blame. I say the *name*, for the *spirit* of the
christian religion is as much in opposition to
such practices, as it is to the practice of war.
What has become of torture in courts of
justice, so called, and of the rack, and the
wheel, on which writhed the quivering limbs
of mangled victims? Where are now astrol-
ogy, alchemy, and the like delusions? Light
has shone on public opinion, and the delusions have vanished. And even our own
dear New England, the land of the pilgrims
who fled from persecution, has not escaped
delusion. We shudder to think that only
131 years ago, more than twenty innocent
victims suffered death as *witches*, and many
others were condemned to the same fate.

The *present generation* has witnessed a
wonderful change in public opinion. A few
years ago one or two solitary individuals,
whose names will brighten the page of his-

tory, raised their voices against the slave
trade; and it is now nearly abolished, and
held in as great detestation as piracy. And
we have reason to think, that the time is not
far distant, when the holding of our fellow
creatures in bondage will be considered as
great a crime, as the act of reducing them
to slavery.

If so great changes have taken place in
public opinion, why may we not expect others; and that the time may come, when
the practice of war will be viewed by all civilized nations with as much abhorrence, as
any of the practices I have mentioned.

NO. 3.

Ostensible causes of War.

In attempting a remedy for sickness, or
any other evil, it is necessary first to investigate the cause. If that can be removed, a
remedy may often be successfully applied.
If it sometimes happens that past evils can
only be deplored; it is certain, future evils
can always be prevented, if we can prevent
the cause.

The question "Whence come wars and
fightings among you ?" has been asked and
answered in Holy Writ. Every war which
has desolated the earth, may be traced to
the "lust" of applause, power, gold, revenge, or some other lust equally vile; and
we need only to look at the manifestos of

belligerents to see, that they reciprocally charge each other with these motives.

The causes of war may be arranged under two general heads; viz. *ostensible* and *real.*

I shall endeavor to show that, even according to the declarations and avowals of the belligerents themselves, seven eighths of the wars, which have afflicted mankind, have had their origin in *folly* and *wickedness;* and if we duly consider the *real* causes of wars, we shall find that at least nineteen twentieths have originated in *ambition* and *avarice.*

In considering the ostensible causes of war, I avail myself of the third report of the committee of inquiry instituted by the Mass. Peace Society.   " In the report, the inquiry is confined to wars, in which civilized nations have been engaged, since they became christian, or since Constantine assumed the reins of the Roman empire: omitting a great number of petty wars, in small nations of antiquity,—temporary insurrections, or trivial hostilities—and a multitude of wars, which have been carried on between christian and savage nations, such as the aborigines of Asia and America. The report relates to 286 wars of. magnitude, in which christian nations have been engaged. These are divided into the eleven following classes," viz:

" 44   Wars of ambition to obtain extent of
              country.
  22 Wars for plunder, tribute, &c.
  24 Wars of retaliation or revenge.
   8 Wars to settle some question of honor
              or prerogative.

6 Wars arising from disputed claims to some territory.

41 Wars arising from disputed titles to crowns.

30 Wars commenced under pretence of assisting an ally.

23 Wars originating in jealousy of rival greatness.

5 Wars which have grown out of commerce.

55 Civil Wars.

28 Wars on account of religion, including the crusades against the Turks and heretics."

286

To which may be added the wars which have been waged since the report was made: viz. the war in which Spain is engaged against the liberty of her colonies in America: the war by which Austria extinguished the spark of liberty in Naples; the war in which France is now engaged against the liberty of Spain, and the war in which the Turks are engaged against the liberty of the Greeks.

Let any man, be his prejudices in favor of war ever so great, take his pen and mark out those wars above enumerated, which he thinks *wicked* or *foolish* and how few the remainder! So that the most bigoted partizan of war must acknowledge, that, at least in nine cases out of ten, the party making war has been guilty of murder and robbery.

I leave the consideration of the remedy—
which is more or less in every man's hands—
until I come to consider the *real* causes of
war; which I purpose to do, in my next communication.

NO. 4.

Real causes of War.

In my last communication I mentioned
the ostensible causes of war, gathered from
the declaration and manifestos of belligerents and arranged under eleven distinct
heads.   But I think the real and secret causes of war may be always found in these four
vices, viz. love of power, lust of praise,
thirst for gold, and desire of revenge. These
are the hidden motives which actuate rulers
and people, deceivers and deceived; but not
equally, for sometimes one motive predomi-
nates, and sometimes another; yet they are
all found to influence the various classes of
society, when a nation is preparing for offensive war. The sovereign wants to extend
his power; the general pants for military
fame; the statesman wants money or patronage; and the people are led to fancy some
injury is done to them, or else some insult is
purposely offered to another state with a sure
expectation of retaliation. Impediments are
artfully thrown in the way of an amicable
adjustment, and prince and people, soldiers
and citizens, rush on their own destruction.
Famine, pestilence, poverty, misery and an-

guish ensue. The people, feeling what they
would not foresee, are clamorous for peace,
and the " *status ante bellum*" succeeds. The
prince has extended his power *over his own
subjects;* the statesman has shared with the
contractor the people's money; the general
has acquired his laurels; the people have
had their revenge! and all set about recruiting for another struggle.

But the passions are not *confined* to the
classes with which I have connected them.
The prince or ruler often wants money to
squander on his pleasures; and the people
never pay so readily as when they are gratifying their revenge. The statesman wants
more power, as well as money. The general often gathers gilded laurels, and the people are in love with military fame, or covet
some neighboring province.

War creates a vast number of new and lu-
crative offices, and thus increases the power
and influence of the ruler and his favorites.
The idle and dissolute find a support in the
army; war becomes their trade and occupa-
tion. Bread is taken from the mouth of labor to support the indolent. If the people
too late see their error, and demand a peace,
they are treated as rebels; and the arms
which have been purchased with the fruits
of their labor are turned against them; for
war and liberty do not flourish together.
War is the time to abrogate charters and
change constitutions; which, if not entirely
destroyed, are often so weakened by dan-

2*

gerous precedents, as to be always afterward "a rope of sand," "a nose of wax." When the enemy have made an inroad into the country, the people think little of an encroachment on the constitution. Methods which may appear best in the present exigency are preferred, without regard to the future. A nation may come out of what is called a glorious and successful war, with an injury to its constitution which all its glory and conquests will never countervail.

It is evident that the beginning of a war depends on the will of the people, even under arbitrary governments: for the most despotic princes cannot make war with any hope of success, without the consent of their subjects. Sometimes indeed a majority of their subjects who are fit to bear arms, are soldiers; then the prince can do his pleasure, and dreadful must be the state of the peasantry. But under limited monarchies and republican governments, it is certain that rulers cannot go to war without the consent of the people. The people will seldom or never give their consent, unless they are deceived by their rulers, or their passions, or both. It is evident then that the continuance of war depends on public opinion; and that every individual in a free country has in this respect a solemn and sacred duty to perform. He can withhold his approbation, when the question on going to war is actually before him; he can contrib-

ute to the diffusion of correct principles,
which may influence his fellow citizens for
ages to come.

NO. 5.

Desire of extension of Territory a cause of War.

LEAVING the predatory excursions of savages and half civilized nations out of the question, we find that under despotic governments, the most frequent object of war is extension of territory. Of the 286 wars, mentioned in my third communication, which
have desolated the christian world since the
days of Constantine, those which have been
professedly undertaken for conquest amount
to 44. This is a greater number than belongs
to any other of the eleven classes, except
civil wars, which originate from various causes.   But if we take into consideration all
the wars which have been waged by despotic
princes from the earliest times, it is probable
that a love of power in the prince *has been*
the most frequent cause of war; yet often
this love of power in the despot has been
cherished by the general, who wished to acquire military fame—by the minister, who
wished to make himself necessary and advance his favorites,—and by the courtier,
who wished to share the plunder.

The love of power is, in princes, so inti-
mately connected with love of fame, that it
is difficult to distinguish in all cases the one

from the other.—" Macedonia's madman and
the Swede" conquered nations, not altogether
for the purpose of extending their power, for
they gave away kingdoms with a lavish hand;
Alexander's chief motive was a love of fame;
while Charles seemed to take a brutal delight
in havoc and bloodshed.   Frederic III,* false-
ly called the great, partook of both characters;
and while it is difficult to say which moved
him most, a love of power, or a love of fame,
it is evident he loved war for its own sake.
The reasons he himself gave, for the invasion
of a neighboring country were, " an army
quite fit to march ; a treasury ready prepared ; and perhaps the ambition of acquiring
renown."   These were his avowed reasons
for robbing the daughter of Charles VI. of
one of her finest provinces ; and such was
the man whom the world calls *the great.*   I
cannot now stop to particularize some of the
actions of these great robbers ; and would
barely observe, that, as far as these conquerors were actuated by public opinion, it was
in the power of the public to restrain their
ambition and cupidity.

In exposing the baseness of monarchs or
republics, that make war for the *express* purpose of extending their territories, I feel that

---

* He was the grandson of Frederic Flector of Bran-
denburg. and first King of Prussia. and son of Frederic
William. The English writers call him Frederic the
the III. and his father (Frederic William) Frederic II.
while the French writers call him Frederic II. and his father Frederic William 1st. It is to this uncertainty as
much as to his royal robberies that he owes the epithet of
great.

I have but little to do. Even the same Frederic, on his invasion of Silesia, felt himself constrained, by a deference to public opinion, to " erase the word *Deo** from the motto of his standard in which it was joined with *pro patria.*"† No nation now makes war *professedly* for the purpose of extending its limits. So far peace principles have already triumphed ; and it is certainly a great inducement to the friends of peace, to persevere. But in our own age we have seen a mighty conqueror overrun kingdoms, and subdue empires, and extirpate republics ; not indeed with the *avowed* purpose of enlarging his dominions. But no one doubts that he loved power as much as fame, and we have heard this man styled *the great ;* as though no man could be great, unless he were a great robber. Nor are individuals alone to be charged with robberies on a great scale. Nations, and even republics, share the disgrace. I blush for my own country, when I remember, how publicly the hope of extending our limits, both north and south, has been urged as a cause of war. Very happily for us, we did not conquer the provinces we fough᷑ for : though we did obtain those for which we negotiated. *These* we may expect to retain peaceably ; the *others* would have been a bone of contention for ages.

It may be needless, in this enlightened age, to expatiate on the baseness of the wretch,

* God.   † For country.

who, for the sake of his own personal gratification and aggrandizement, scatters death and
misery among an unoffending people; or compare him to the assassin, highwayman, or in-
cendiary, who acts on similar principles.
Yet, so long as many are found, who bestow
their unqualified praise on such characters,
it is evident, they approve their conduct and
would imitate it if in their power. It is the
duty, then, of every friend of man, on all
proper occasions, openly to express his detestation of such characters. For my own
part, I would as soon place the bust of a
noted highwayman on my mantle piece, as I
would that of a conqueror. Both are robbers, and I see no reason, why the great robber should be more honored than the less,
except that he is more eminently wicked.

NO. 6.

On the patriotism of Conquerors.

To trace the course of conquerors, and observe the effects of their conquests on their
own dominions, may gratify our curiosity.·
To observe their motives, and to discriminate
between their love of their own glory, and
their pretended love of country, may correct
some of our erroneous opinions.

Philip, by bribery and force, conquered all
Greece, and raised the little state of Macedon
to an elevated rank among the nations. Alexander succeeded him. By his address and
his power, he stirred up the Greeks to re-

venge on the Persians the invasion of Xerxes, which had taken place more than one hundred and fifty years before. All Greece is precipitated on Asia. He passes the Granicus, conquers Persia, marches an army across the Lybian desert, to visit the temple of Jupiter Ammon, and gets himself declared the son of that sheepheaded god, not much to the credit of his mother's chastity. Returning, he conquers what was then called the world—at one time lamenting that he had not, like Achilles, a Homer to trumpet his fame, and afterwards crying, like a spoiled child, because he had not another world to conquer; or rather, because his soldiers would not cross the Ganges and leave the world he had already conquered. Of what advantage is all this to Macedon? It is in the mean time governed by a deputy, who is expelled by the intrigues of two women, who divide and govern his paternal dominions. Very few Macedonians ever return home; and Macedon, instead of becoming the mistress, becomes a province of the conquered empire. The Greeks degenerated to Persians, and after the conqueror's death,— occasioned by debauch or poison——play " strange funeral games" in honor of his memory, covering the world with havoc and bloodshed, while contending with each other in dividing the spoil. Thus we see Persia ruined on account of the unsuccessful invasion of Greece, and Greece ruined by the successful invasion of Persia. But can any one suppose, that love of country was Alexander's motive for this invasion ? Was it not his own unbounded ambition ? And would such ambition exist, if mankind did not give their applause to such characters ?

Charles XII of Sweden was early trained to martial enterprises ; and by reading the history of Alexander, he became inflamed with a desire of imitating his exploits. "The Swedes too, after the example of their king, were seized with an enthusiasm for military glory, that allowed but little time for reflection. Taxes, which are the sinews of war, were considered, and readily granted, as an honorary tribute, and every family was ambitious of furnishing a soldier." Charles fought like a tiger ; gained many victories ; humbled the king of Denmark ; dethroned the king of Poland ; and invaded Russia. At Pultowa the scale turned, and his own army was destroyed, and he fled almost alone into Turkey; whence he returned to renew the war, and invaded Norway. There, happily for his country, he was killed by a random shot from a Danish battery, or assassinated by his French aid ; it is uncertain and immaterial which. But what fruits did his country reap from his victories ? The flower of his yeomanry were destroyed in the wars ; famine threatened ; pestilence always follows famine. A part of his kingdom was ceded to the Czar, and Sweden has not yet recovered her strength. Whatever his pretensions to patriotism might have been, love of military glory

and of bloodshed, were his ruling passions.
What fanned that love of glory? It was reading the encomiums which historians had lav-
ished on the character of Alexander. Every
man who praises such characters, becomes
accessary to their crimes.

Our limits allow us to notice but one more
of these conquerors—these " rods of God's
anger." Was the love of Corsica or of
France the leading motive with Napoleon?
Was it for patriotism, that he marched his
army to the burning deserts of Egypt, and
frozen forests of Russia? No, his own power
and glory, and the aggrandizement of his
family, were his motives. But the French
shared his military glory. Let it be granted;
will that repay the heart-rending pangs of
the parents, the widows and orphans of the
hundreds of thousands of miserable conscripts
who fell at Borodina, Beresina, and Waterloo? of those who withered under the scorch-
ing sun and pestilential air of Egypt, or sunk
benumbed with cold and hunger, beneath the
inclement skies of Russia? to say nothing of
the sufferings of those they attacked; of
towns in flames; of kingdoms desolated; of
famine and pestilence stalking in their rear;
or of prisoners murdered in cold blood; or
of sick and wounded soldiers poisoned by order of their own general. All for what?
For military glory. And what is military
glory? A puff, a breath, which every individual can increase or diminish: and every individual is accountable for the part he takes

3

in inflating military pride. When conquerors shall no longer be eulogized, the race will become extinct; for they live, like the fabled vampyre, on the breath of the people.

NO. 7.

Love of fame a cause of War.

IN tracing the *causes* of war we shall find, that the *love of fame* stands foremost, and is of all others the most frequent, the most universal, the most plausible, and, like

——*" Aaron's serpent, swallows up the rest."*

When a sovereign makes war professedly for the love of power, he meets with general, —I wish I could say universal—detestation. When the love of wealth is the prominent motive, the execration is still more general; and we see that but five Wars, out of the two hundred and eighty six I have mentioned, have grown out of commerce. Though, without doubt, revenge is often a motive for war, it is seldom or never avowed; and wars of retaliation are always called wars of self-defence. But when a prince, or a republic, makes war for glory, glory is always claimed.—Every victory is glory; a good retreat is glory; and some are so sagacious in hunting out glory, that they find it even in a defeat. This same glory is a sticking kind of stuff. None ever rubs off. Ask Britain, what compensates her for her myriads of lives lost, and her thousand millions of debt?

She answers, *glory.* Ask France, what she
obtained by her wars, to compensate her for
the hundreds of thousands of her subjects destroyed by cold and heat, pestilence and famine, fire and sword? She answers, *glory.*
Ask ourselves what we obtained by our late
war of retaliation? The answer is *glory,
glory, glory.* But what is this glory, which
seems to be a panacea, to cure all evils and
heal all wounds? Especially, what is this
military glory? What is it, but "a puff of
noisy breath?" Will it smooth the dying pil-
low, or give one drop of water to cool the
tongue? What is there in a love of glory to
raise it above the love of money, or a love of
pleasure? Is it not as selfish as either; and
does it not produce more crimes than both?
It is more exclusive and more envious than
either. The rich envy not the rich: men of
pleasure love their like: but Alexander envi-
ed the dead Achilles, and no conqueror can
bear a rival. Yet the love of glory gilds the
blackest crimes. Let a man lie, deceive and
murder for money, and he is called an execrable wretch. Let a man commit forgery,
deceive his antagonist, draw him into an ambuscade, or an unfavorable position, and then
murder him; if glory be the motive, honor
is the reward: if money be the object, the reward is a halter. Although a blinded and
depraved world may reward one with a statue, and the other with a gibbet, He who "tri-
eth the heart and searcheth the reins" will
reward both alike. What is a crime in an

individual is a crime in a nation—for nations
are composed of individuals: and they cannot hope to divide the glory, without sharing
the guilt. A murder committed by an individual, a crew, or an army, is still a murder:
and that, whether the motive be plunder, or
glory, or revenge. The individual robber,
the crew of pirates, are hung and gibbeted.
The hero, the army, and the nation, under
similar circumstances, are glorified.

Individuals, when carrying on war on their
own account, often pretend that the glory of
their country is their object. Patriotism is
a fine-sounding word, and "covers a multitude of sins." But grant for a moment, that
his country's glory is the leading motive with
the general, the admiral, or the privateers-
man; and that neither of them is seeking his
own individual honor or wealth; and that he
would rather lose both, than his country's
fame should suffer: allowing all this, it only
extends selfishness to a little wider circle, of
which the centre remains the same. It is *my*
country,—"may she always be successful,
right or wrong"—a sentiment which has
been much applauded in this country; but
which, to my ear, sounds like a privateers-
man's encouragement to his crew—"board
her, my boys; a rich prize, friend or foe."
How different from this is that charity which
"suffereth long and is kind; envieth not;
vaunteth not itself; is not puffed up; seeketh
not her own; rejoiceth not in iniquity; bear-
eth all things; endureth all things." Can a

christian *consistently* rejoice for the success
of his country, in an unjust war?—then he
can rejoice in his own success in an iniqui-
tous and oppressive law suit, or in midnight
depredations—which is as much as to say,
he can be a christian, and not be guided by
christian principles. The man, whoever he
may be, who can give glory to his own nation, or any other, for victories obtained in
an unjust war, is in heart guilty of all the
crimes committed in that war: and is in fact
one cause of all the misery which war occasions.

NO. 8.

Avarice a cause of War.

A LOVE of money, covetousness of others'
goods, or avarice as it is commonly called,
has been a frequent cause of war. This case
has been much more frequent among barba-
rians, than among civilized nations, as far as
it relates to rulers ; but perhaps not more frequent, in relation to the nation at large. It
is true, war is a good excuse for raising taxes ; but despotic monarchs want no such excuse, and in limited monarchies and free
governments, the rulers,—though they may
enrich themselves, as individuals,—certainly
impoverish themselves as a government. No
war, in modern times, pays its expenses ; but
on the contrary leads the belligerent nation
with debt. It is not among rulers, especially
arbitrary rulers, that we are to look for the
3*

operation of avarice, in causing war. It is
among the *people*, from the highest to the
lowest, including rulers only in their individual capacity. A minister, bringing on a war,
thereby increases his power and his opportu-
nities of enriching himself, his friends, his
relatives and dependents, by increasing his
patronage. Military and naval characters
expect pay, plunder and glory. Privateers-
men have an opportunity of robbing with
impunity. Manufacturers of arms, gunpow-
der and ardent spirits hope to sell their com-
modities. Even the mechanic who makes
the leather cap and belt ; the tailor, who cuts
out the soldier's clothes ; and the seamstress,
who makes them up ; each one expects " his
gain from his quarter." The body politic
resembles a dead carcase, surrounded by
hawks and vultures, of all sects and sizes
and descriptions, each carrying off with glee
his reeking mouthful of plunder ; so that a
year of war,—beside exposing coasts and
commerce to the depredations of the enemy,
—consumes the revenues of many years.
Unhappily for the cause of peace, a way has
been found out, to divide among the present
generation, the property of posterity and to
riot on future harvests. By means of national credit, an unnatural abundance of
money is generated, in time of war ; and future generations are sent supperless to bed.
The British nation now groans under the
weight of taxes occasioned by the warlike
character of former rulers ; and the sins of

the fathers are visited on "the children to the third and fourth generation." Let my country take warning, if she would preserve her liberty, and her happiness. War is an enemy to both.

I cannot dismiss this subject, without considering a character, now, happily, not so common as in former times. I mean the soldier by trade—a professed fighter, who enters any service, where he gets the best pay, or where he has the greatest prospect of plunder, or of distinction and promotion. In what does this character differ from the hired assassin? Does one stab for pay?— so does the other. Does one murder in the dark?—does not the other consider stratagem, ambuscade, the mine, and even the torpedo, as honorable warfare? Whatever distinction man may make between the two characters, "the Judge of all the earth will do right." Nor is this execrable character peculiar to him, who leaves his own country, to find employment as a man-slayer abroad. The man who engages in *any* war, and slaughters his fellow-man, for the sole object of pay or plunder, is no better than a highwayman,—unless we view him in the character of a hangman or public executioner—if he murders for honor and renown. he is still as selfish as the other; and if the fame and honor of his country be his motive, it is still but an extended selfishness.

I do not mean to insinuate, that there have not been those who have followed the trade

of war, who were noble, frank and generous,
in every thing unconnected with their profession; and forward to relieve the sufferings,
and assuage the anguish, which they had
been instrumental in causing. I have known
many naval, and some military characters,
both at home and abroad, and have found
most of them amiable in their dispositions,
and gentlemanly in their manners. How
can we account for it, that a man, naturally
tender-hearted and affectionate, should be induced by pay plunder or glory, to cause
the keenest anguish, and the most severe af-
flictions to those who never injured him, and
never knew him—to break the lover's heart,
to make the widow's tear to flow, the or-
phan's sighs to ascend to heaven, and the
mother's bosom to heave with unutterable
woe ? I take the reason of these inconsisten-
cies to be this—*men form their judgment of
what is right or wrong, from public opinion,
and not from the word of God.* What public
opinion sanctions, they think just—whatever
it praises, they think laudable. Thus one,
who perhaps was a kind father, and a friend
of the poor, has dashed the blazing fagot in
the face of the half-consumed martyr. Thus
the amiable and benevolent John Newton,
commanded a slave ship, after he had a
good hope that he was a free man in Christ.
Public opinion sanctioned the nefarious traffic ; and no sooner did the signals announce
the arrival of a slave ship off The Rock,
than all the church bells of Liverpool chimed

to the joyful tune of "*welcome home Guinea-man*," something like a modern triumph. What a change has been wrought in public opinion, as it respects the slave trade! The time is not far distant, when the trade of war will be equally execrated; and it is the duty of every one to do what he can, to forward so desirable a consummation.

NO. 9.

Revenge a cause of War.

THE only remaining cause of war, which we purposed to consider, is *revenge*. The more barbarous the nation, the more frequently is this diabolical passion exhibited. Among civilized nations it generally takes the name of retaliation, and sometimes of self-defence:—but the thing is the same, by whatever name it is called. This passion, like avarice, is seldom found in the breasts of rulers, unless their own personal dignity has been assailed: but the excuse is often used by them, when they wish to raise the passions of their people to the war pitch. Then injuries are sought for and generally found; and if not found, are easily provoked. Then ambition and avarice find excuse for the war whoop; and a nation arrogates to itself the prerogative of Him who has said, "Vengeance is mine." But on whom do they vent their revenge?—not one time in a hundred, on those from whom they received the injury. Is a merchant vessel captured or the national

flag insulted ? The property of some innocent merchant is plundered, in retaliation;
or a neighboring province is invaded, and
peaceable husbandmen are driven from their
ploughs ; their fields are ravaged, their houses burnt, and their flocks slaughtered. It is
true this kind of retaliation falls less severely
on the innocent than formerly ; thanks to
the prevalence of peace principles :—the day
will come, when they shall altogether escape.
—Is a citizen impressed and held in bondage ? We avenge the injury, by subjecting
thousands of our citizens to a similar fate ;
and by their means inflict our vengeance on
those, who are suffering a like calamity ; or
on others, who are equally innocent, and are
as much adverse to impressment as we are.
True, we do not kill our prisoners, like the
polished Athenians : but we keep them in
prison, until we return them back to the
same masters to whom they were before in
bondage ; and we continue to sacrifice thousands of lives and millions of property to
punish those who never injured us ; and be-
tray more folly than the child, who vents his
anger on the rod by which he has been whip-
ped. Finally, when we have sacrificed thousands of our own citizens, and slain thousands of our enemy, and have expended
more than our whole mercantile capital for
the protection of some disputed right of commerce, we have glutted our revenge, and sit
down contented with the loss : and if any regret remain, we are reminded of the *glory* we

have gained, and that reconciles us to all our losses.

But the losses of seamen and of commerce are not the only evils which a nation increases by an attempt to avenge them. Instances are numerous, both in ancient and modern history, of nations bringing on themselves evils, tenfold greater than those, of which they complain, and of the same nature. To instance but one of many; we may notice the war which the Lacedemonians waged against the Messenians, to avenge the violation of some of their females, at a temple on the borders of the two countries. But Rollin suspects, that "a desire of extending their dominions, and of seizing a country which lay so convenient for them, might be the *true* cause of war." This "desire of extending their dominions" might have influenced their *kings*, while a desire of revenge might have influenced the *people;*— no uncommon case. However that may be, the war lasted 20 years and nearly destroyed both nations. The Lacedemonians had bound themselves by an oath, not to return to Sparta, until they had made themselves masters of all the cities and lands belonging to the Messenians—in consequence of which they had to take measures to insure to Sparta a succeeding generation, which delicacy forbids me to relate; but which were a thousand times more shameful, and more obnoxious to chastity, than the injuries they pretended to have sustained. I say *pretended;*

for, if I recollect rightly, the Messenians, as
is often the case, denied the charge. The
children which were the fruits of this dis-
graceful commerce were called Partheniatæ;
a name given them to denote the infamy of
their birth. "As soon as they were grown
up, not being able to endure such an oppro-
brious distinction, they banished themselves
from Sparta with one consent," and thus
disappointed the expectations of those *patri-
otic* defenders of chastity.

Wars of revenge are not peculiar to Pagans. The *nominal* disciples of him, who
taught both by precept and example, to return good for evil, have often made war for
which revenge has been the only pretext;
and that sometimes for very trivial injuries.
I mention three instances only, taken from
the Friend of Peace.

"In the year 1005, some soldiers of the
commonwealth of Modena ran away with a
bucket, from a public well, belonging to the
state of Bologna. The implement might be
worth a shilling: but it produced a quarrel,
which was worked up into a long and bloody
war. Henry, king of Sardinia, assisted the
Modenese to keep possession of the bucket,
and in one of the battles he was made pris-
oner." "After twenty-two years' imprison-
ment, he pined away and died."

"Frederic the great gives an account of a
war between England and Spain, which originated from cutting off the ears of an English smuggler. In an old history of the

kings of England, we have seen an account
of a war between that country and France,
the cause of which was this: one boy called
another boy the " son of a bastard;" as this
reproach was founded in fact, it was "worked up into a bloody war." One of the boys
was son to the king of England; the other
to the king of France. The two kings engaged in the quarrel of the two boys, and
thus the two nations were involved in a sanguinary contest."

" We might doubtless collect hundreds of
instances of public wars between christian
nations, which had their origin in occurrences as trivial as the three which have now
been mentioned; and in such wanton wars
millions of lives have been sacrificed. With
men who glory in war, and have been educated to this execrable employment, any
thing will serve for a pretext. However
frivolous it may be in the outset, these manufacturers can soon blow it up into a just and
necessary war, which shall involve myriads
in death or wretchedness."

Alas! when will christians learn, that it
is more noble to forgive an injury, than to
avenge it—that it is more easy to get redress
by negotiation, than by war,—and that it is
unjust to punish the innocent, instead of the
guilty?

4

NO. 10.

Warlike ambition or a love of military glory.

I HAVE in my former numbers taken under consideration, one after another, the *four vices* which are the secret causes of almost all wars; viz: *love of power, lust of praise, thirst for gold*, and *desire of revenge.* Though much might be said under each head, I think it unnecessary to enlarge at present on any but lust of praise, or *love of glory;* which I consider as by far the greatest cause of war, and against which it behoves my fellow citizens to be most on their guard.

It is but a work of supererogation to expose the baseness of the wretch, who sells his country for gold; because mankind are united in the detestation of such characters, and not because such characters have been rare. History informs us of even a king, viz. Charles 2d of England, who was *bribed* by Lewis 14th for a sum agreed on for the *private* use of Charles, to plunge the nation into a destructive war with the Dutch; while Lewis was meditating the conquest of England. We hear also of other kings and emperors who are *subsidized*, or in plain language *bribed* to enter on wars which they might as well avoid. Instances have been too numerous of Grand Viziers, ministers, and even rulers in elective governments, who, to enrich themselves, bring the calamity of war on their country. Nor is it much

more necessary to expose the wickedness of
those, who, for the hope of plunder, pay or
profit, urge their country to war. *The desire of revenge* whenever it is avowed as a
cause of war, (which is indeed seldom,) is
generally detested; though instances could
be adduced, where nations have been involved in the horrors of war, to revenge a fan-
cied affront to a king's mistress or minion.
But those who are actuated by such motives
generally make patriotism and self-defence
a pretext for a war which they have been
instrumental in kindling, for the purpose of
gratifying the basest passions. The *love of
power and dominion* is not so much reprobat-
ed as it deserves; and the extension of territory, by seizing neighboring provinces, is
often put into the scale against murder and
robbery, havoc and desolation. It is true, a
love of power and dominion is never avowed
by rulers as a cause of war; and the people
generally endeavor to deceive themselves
and others as to the motives by which they
are governed, when they support their rulers
in their unjust aggressions.

Unhappily a *lust of praise* knows no blush,
although it is as selfish and as wicked as any
other lust. Many like Frederic the Great,
are not ashamed to avow, that the "ambition of acquiring renown" has induced them
to invade a neighboring kingdom, and mark
their course with fire and sword; killing all
who oppose them, and giving up the weaker
sex to the lust of an unbridled soldiery, and

condemning old age and infancy to famine, pestilence and death. The love of glory has been the cause of nineteen out of twenty, of the wars which have afflicted the human race. Ambition is the first of all sins in order of time, the greatest of all in extent, and the most mischievous of all in its consequences. It preceded the fall of Adam, and caused war in Heaven. By it our first parents fell; it pervades the world, and is inseparable from our depraved nature. It is a passion which mankind are not ashamed openly to avow, and which parents and teachers diligently foster in youth; though it is directly contrary to the precepts of the gospel. It is true, that emulation does not *always* shew its bad effects, and possibly in some instances may be turned to good account; though it is dangerous to tamper with it. But the ambition of *military* glory has caused more misery and anguish in the world; and has been the parent of more crimes, than all the other vices; and instead of being idolized, as it is by mankind, ought to be execrated.

It is evident, if mankind withheld their applause from military ambition, that the love of glory would cease to be a cause of war; and consequently that, by removing the greatest cause, the greatest part of wars would be prevented. I purpose therefore not to enlarge at present on the other causes of war; but if your patience holds out, to investigate in some future numbers the ex-

citing causes of this love of military glory,
and to consider some of those circumstances
of custom and education which tend to blow
the latent spark into a flame. I am convinced that on due consideration many will find
themselves accessary to murder and rapine,
who have now but little thought of it; and
that all may find they have very much neglected their duty.

NO. 11.

The present system of education a cause of Warlike ambition.

THE course of education from infancy to
manhood at present pursued, tends to inspire
the mind with military ardor, and a *love of
glory*. Almost as soon as a boy is born, care
is taken to give his mind a military turn.
The first playthings given him are miniature
guns, trumpets and drums, with pewter soldiers and wooden swords. Ah fond mother!
little do you think, while you dress the head
of your forward urchin with the paper cap,
and arm him with some mock instruments of
death, and delight to see him march round
your parlor to a military tune, affecting the
manners of the soldier, little do you think, that
you are giving his tender mind a wrong direction, and making impressions which may
last forever—and which, if they do not cause
your own heart to throb with anguish at the
news of his untimely death, may make some
one, who loves her children as well as you

4*

do yours, lament an only son slain by yours, in consequence of the early impressions you have made on his mind ; or may cause some widow to lament the untimely fate of the idol of her heart, whose death may be the effect of your indiscretion.

As soon as the boys leave the lap of their mothers, and begin to play out of doors, the first plaything they have, if in a seaport, is a miniature man of war. If they live in the country, some old pistol barrel is mounted to imitate a field-piece. In both town and country, but most in towns, boys are encouraged to form themselves into *infantry* companies, to shoulder wooden guns, and to elect officers.

The first pictures which are presented to the youthful eye, are of sieges, and battles, and naval engagements, in which, " the pomp and circumstance of glorious war" are portrayed in lively colors. The youth, conscious of his own safety, fancies he sees the fire and smoke, hears the neighing and prancing of horses, the report of cannon and small arms, the clangor of the trumpets, the deep and thrilling tones of martial music, and the shouts of victory. He feels a sensation he can neither describe nor account for, and longs to be in the conflict. If he sees a statue, it is generally that of some great warrior, in military habiliments, trampling on a fallen enemy. The productions of the pencil and chisel always represent to a nation its victories, and never its defeats. These would

tend to allay, as much as those to inflame
military ardor.

Almost all the great processions, which a
boy sees, are of a military nature. He at-
tends the musters, reviews, and sham fights.
His infant mind is inflamed by the splendor
of the uniforms, the glitter of the accoutrements, the pomp and parade of military evo-
lutions, and martial music; and he feels a
strong desire to be an actor in the scène.
He has an idea of the dangers of war, sufficient to make it interesting; but not enough
to disgust. Our rage for military display is
carried so far in this state, that even our processions at academical exhibitions and college commencements are marshalled by an
officer with a drawn sword and sash; and
our reverend fathers, the faculty, trustees,
overseers, clergy, &c. only want a musket
and knapsack, to transform them into a company of militia.

As soon as boys are able to read, especially if intended for a liberal education, the
books which are put into their hands are
heathen authors, who exalt warlike heroes
above the skies. And, as if done on purpose
to cherish a war spirit, the peaceful Geor-
gics of Virgil are generally passed over, and
the martial characters of the Æneid are held
up to his admiration. I appeal to every man of
education to say, if the reading of the Greek
and Latin classics has not excited in him
a passion to imitate the heroes of ancient
times; and if the martial scenes so ably por-

trayed by the poets have not accompanied his
sleeping and waking dreams; so that he has
felt like young Themistocles, when "the tro-
phies of Miltiades would not suffer him to
sleep." This state of feeling is much applauded by a writer in the Spectator, probably Addison; and by many is considered as
the very "beau ideal" of heroism. I must
confess myself of a different opinion; and
that all this fair outside show of war, in my
mind, resembles the fruit, by which, according to Milton, the fallen angels were condemned to be repeatedly deceived.

> ———" Greedily they pluck'd
> The fruitage fair to sight.
> ——they, fondly thinking to allay
> Their appetite with gust, instead of fruit,
> Chew'd bitter ashes, which the offended taste
> With spattering noise rejected; oft they assay'd,
> Hunger and thirst constraining; drugg'd as oft,
> With hatefullest disrelish writh'd their jaws,
> With soot and cinders filled."

At eighteen years of age, our youth is
made to shoulder a musket, and appear
" armed at all points" at a rendezvous; which
is generally at or near a *grog-shop*, where he
may learn to get drunk, swear and fight, and
thus complete his education.

A nation thus educated is no more capable of judging on the subject of war, than the
inhabitants of Georgia are capable of judging
on the question of slavery. The difference
of opinion on the subject of slavery in Maine
and in Georgia is principally the effect of
education. So is the difference of opinion

,een the present generation and former
.es on the subject of the inquisition and ju-
dicial combat. I have no doubt that many
who have burned heretics or flogged slaves,
have possessed as much natural benevolence
as those who encourage war. They had the
vices of their age and country; and I have as
little doubt that the time will soon come,
when the custom of war will be as odious as
intolerance and slavery. Let parents do as
much to educate their children in the principles of peace, as has been done to inflame
their minds with a love of war—let the turpi-
tude and brutality of those who seek for glory in blood and tears and groans, be so exposed that the Alexanders, the Cæsars, the
Frederics, and the Napoleons shall cease to
be objects of emulation; and " wars and
fightings will cease throughout the earth."
It is the duty of every mother, of every
father, and of every instructer of youth to educate children in a manner very different
from the prevailing custom. It is the duty
of every individual, of both sexes and of all
ages; but especially is it incumbent on public teachers, to hold up to general execration,
the guilty destroyers of the human race. At
least it is their duty, on all suitable occasions,
to give their testimony against the custom of
war. Those who neglect this duty are
chargeable with conniving at murder and
robbery; but "he who saith unto the wicked,
Thou art righteous; him shall the people
curse; nations shall abhor him."

NO. 12.

The militia system a cause of Warlike ambition.

AMONG the customs, which in this country excite a love of military glory, may be reckoned the militia system. The advocates of a militia in time of peace, so far from denying this, give it as one of their reasons why every man should be a soldier. The standing military committee of the house of representatives of New Hampshire, to whom was referred so much of Gov. Woodbury's message, in June last, as related to the militia, in a very lengthy report—in which they commend the present system and oppose a change recommended by the Governor—say: "To lessen the number of company trainings, or regimental musters, would destroy that *military ardor*, that high and honorable pride among officers, without which our militia would cease to exist. The committee are sensible of the considerations which induce individuals to accept offices of trust and honor in the militia, the discharge of the duties of which is attended with the sacrifice of so much time and treasure." Thus we see by the confession of the professed advocates of the militia system, that it tends to foster a warlike spirit, which invites aggression; and gives our young men a taste and relish for war, by exhibiting only the fair side, and thus induces them to sup

port war measures and war men, which in
republican countries has a great effect in
bringing on war.   By the tenor of the whole
report, war seems to be the ultimate object
of the supporters of the militia system.   I
think it would be well to treat these high
spirited gentry in the same manner as the
Indians do their young chiefs, when they
are seized with a war fever, which would
endanger the nation.   On such occasions
the old Sachems take the hot-headed young
fellows to a cool brook; and with shells or
sharp stones, so scratch and lacerate their
bodies, as to reduce their blood and cool
their courage.   The difficulty with us is, that
the old Sachems are as hot-headed as the
young chiefs.

The second sentence of the quotation informs us, that "The committee are sensible
of the considerations which induce individuals to accept offices of trust and honor in our
militia."   Now, Sir, what are these motives,
of which this very *sharp sighted* committee
are so *sensible?*   What but pride, ambition,
and a love of distinction so congenial to depraved nature?   This love of distinction,
has however, in this state, defeated its own
object; for our military titles are so common—I had almost said universal—that it
has become an honorable distinction, to be
without a title.   If you meet with a man
whose appearance is below mediocrity, it is
safest to greet him with a military title; for
it is an even chance you are right: but if

you are wrong the other way, and omit the
title, you may unpardonably offend a man
who has nothing else to recommend him.
But so great an honor cannot be obtained
without a *sacrifice*, and the sentence above
quoted concludes thus: " the discharge of
the duties of which is attended with the sacrifice of much *time* and *treasure*." Here we
have the " *quid pro quo*." Here is "time and
treasure" against honor. Who would hesi-
tate to make the *glorious* choice ? What is
time to an immortal being ? And as for that
trash called treasure, how can it be better
expended than in epaulets, lace and sword
hilts, where an ounce of silver or gold would
make an infinitely greater display, than it
would in an endorsement on a note, or the
support of religion. As for the treasure expended in treating inferiors, certainly it
tends to raise their spirits and inflame their
martial ardor. Besides, the State gets, or
might get, a great part of the price of the
liquor, in impost, excise, and tax on licences;
and so the " sinews of war" are strengthened,
while the spirit of war is exhilarated. I have
heard a general officer in this State declare,
that he had expended nine hundred dollars
in eleven days of military reviews. I think
he " paid dear for the whistle;" but certainly
he deserves a quantum of honor equal to the
" sacrifice." But seriously, this sacrifice of
time and treasure is a great evil, independently of the intoxication and licentiousness
it occasions. A great number of honest, in-

dependent farmers have been brought to poverty by the indulgence of this militia spirit, and have the honor of driving other men's teams, and tilling other men's fields. The sacrifice of time and treasure in Maine cannot be fairly rated at less than 150,000 dollars per annum. How many Canals would this sum dig? How many Falls would it lock? How many Roads would it make? How many Teachers would it support? How would it convert a natural and moral wilderness into a Paradise?

But the sacrifice of time and treasure is not all the sacrifice which is made to the militia system. The committee dexterously pass over the sacrifice of morals and sobriety, though of infinitely greater importance than the other. Many of our drunkards date their first intoxication at the muster, where the sweetened toddy is lavishly dealt out by all officers, who have a love of militia glory. Apprentices and farmers' sons under age, like very well the sport of getting away from the eye of their masters and parents, to indulge their appetites and passions. To them the sacrifice of time is nothing, and the sacrifice of treasure is only that of a few cents they carry to prolong their intemperate indulgence, or to *treat* their officers, when they think them niggardly in the quantity or quality of their potations;—an insult, which every officer of a proper *spirit*, endeavors to avoid. But those privates, who are not corrupted by the bad examples they are com-

pelled to witness, find, when they become of
age, the militia a most burthensome and oppressive tax.   They are obliged to work
hard to buy their accoutrements, and to
make up the lost time to their employers;
and I have often heard them declare, that
they had rather *work* two days, than *train*
one.   It is true, the members of our legislature represent this matter differently.   But
many of them are themselves officers in the
militia, ambitious, and fond of command;
and so an oppressive system is kept up, contrary to the will of the people; and a sort of
tyranny is exercised in a free country.

It must be granted, that the first settlers
of this country, by their wanton aggressions
on the natives, made the militia system *appa-
rently* necessary, in their time.   Belknap, in
his history of New-Hampshire, observes,
" However fond we may have been of accus-
ing the Indians of treachery and infidelity, it
must be confessed that the example was set
them by the Europeans."   A European voy-
ager by the name of Hunt, who visited the
northern coast of America in 1614, " decoyed
about twenty Indians on board, and sold them
for slaves in Malaga.   This perfidious action
excited a violent jealousy in the natives, and
bitterly enraged them against succeeding adventurers."   This and similar conduct was
the first cause of our militia.   By our own
injustice we provoked the natives, and then
were obliged to be armed and trained for defence and retaliation.   Belknap remarks,

" Had we always treated them (the Indians)
with that justice and humanity which our religion inculcates, we might have lived as much
in harmony with them as with any other people." The correctness of this opinion was
manifested by the Quakers in Pennsylvania,
who never had a war with the Indians, during the seventy years they held the reins of
government in that province. But *our* fore-
fathers first provoked them by injustice, and
then organized a militia to repel and punish
them. Frequently a custom remains, after
its cause has ceased. Our frontier is now
guarded by a line of missionaries, armed only
with " the sword of the Spirit ;" and no hostile note is heard, except where our government have pushed a *military* force far into
the Indian territories. Yet the militia system continues, though the occasion of it has
ceased, and by its burthens and its evil effects, punishes us for the sins of our fore-
fathers.

Were the system answerable to the end
proposed, we might perhaps be more easily
reconciled to the " sacrifice of time and treasure," and morals, which it occasions. It is
continued professedly to " execute the laws,
suppress insurrection, and repel invasion."
The only time, so far as I know, that the
militia has been called out to support the
laws, was by the Governor of Pennsylvania,
to oppose the marshal of the United States.—
This was executing the laws with a vengeance. It was found totally insufficient to

suppress the whiskey insurrection; for nothing can be more absurd than the calling out
of the militia, to suppress insurrection, when
the militia themselves are the insurgents.
How well the militia repelled invasion, let
Maine answer.

To shew that my opinion on this subject
is not singular, I quote the address which
Major General Calvin Jones, of North Carolina, presented, together with his resignation,
to the legislature of that state. " I hazard
nothing by the assertion, that one week of
actual service will do more for discipline,
than the whole life of a man, who is dragged
from his family half a dozen times in the
year to expose his health to the elements,
his awkwardness to the public gaze, and his
morals to the contamination of electioneering
treats.******* No substantial benefits are
obtained, and the injury inflicted on his property and morals are incalculable. ******
These observations are the result of deliber-
ate judgment, formed by all the lights afford-
ed by twenty-four years of experience in
different offices in the militia,—on muster
grounds, in the halcyon days of peace ; and
the tented field, in the stormy season of war.
*****I entered the militia service with the
most sanguine expectations of introducing
reform. ***But the sober lessons of experience have taught me the futility of all such
hopes and attempts, not only here, but in
every state where I have had a knowledge
of the militia." I have heard many military

officers express the same opinion as General
Jones.

It was not my intention, when I commenced this communication, to shew the futility
or the oppression of our militia system, nor
to advert to its demoralizing tendency ; but
barely to shew its connexion with a love of
military glory, as a predisposing cause of
war. The topic is so interesting, that I have
inadvertently strayed from my object ; and as
I have already far exceeded my usual bounds,
and I fear the reader's patience, it is too
late to resume the subject, at least, for the
present.

NO. 13.

Preparation for War often the cause of it.

THERE are certain maxims, which have been
received by the Christian world, as blindly
and implicitly as the " ipse dixit" of the Sta-
gyrite was received by his disciples. " The
Pope is infallible ;" " Ignorance is the mother of devotion :" these were maxims of former
times, which it would have been dangerous
to gainsay. Whosoever would not subscribe
to them was liable to be burned at the stake
or broken on the wheel. They have passed
away, never more to return. But we have
in our day a maxim, which is as blindly and
implicitly avowed, as either of the above ;
and the person who shall presumptuously deny its truth, if not in danger of the fagot
and the rack, must expect contempt and rid-

5*

icule, often more dreaded than either. The maxim referred to is this: " The best way to keep peace is to be always prepared for war." Stubborn facts give the lie to this adage, and in due time it will pass off like others.

On general principles it is obvious, that the greater the preparation for war, and the more military ardor is inflamed, the greater is the provocation to aggression from neighboring nations in self-defence; and the more a nation excites a martial spirit, the more ready is it to engage in war, and purposely provoke aggression. This is the reason why England and France have been so often engaged in cruel and desolating wars, and have sacrificed their millions on the bloody altar of Moloch. Their losses and sufferings have been immense, and the condition of the bulk of their subjects deplorable, and their mutual gains nothing, unless it be glory; though it is difficult to conceive how one power gained glory, unless the other lost. But allowing them all the glory their hearts can wish, what American citizen would wish to exchange his liberty, peace and happiness, for their glory ?

But to return to the subject. I have already, in former numbers, remarked that the reasons which Frederic the third, king of Prussia, gave for his first war, were, that he had a full treasury and an army quite fit to march. All the military preparations of Frederic William, his father, (famous for his

regiment of giants, and his oppression and
parsimony,) so far from securing peace to
his subjects, were the causes—together with
a love of glory—of his states' being involved
in war soon after his death. He left to his
son an army of 60,000 men and an abundant
treasury. With these Frederic the third immediately attacked the queen of Hungary.
In a time of peace he increased his army by
every means in his power, even the most unjust and oppressive; making every man a
soldier, and grinding his subjects by every
method of extortion, until he had raised the
number of his army to 200,000. This, so far
from securing peace, armed against him
France, Austria, Sweden and Russia, who
became jealous of his power and ambition.
Thus the preparation for war became the direct and only cause of war; and the armaments of the Empress Queen, made necessary
by his own, were his only pretext for commencing hostilities. He demanded of her
the intent of her armaments. "Her answer
was not as explicit as he wished, and he immediately commenced hostilities, and involved himself in a long and hazardous war, in
the course of which he acquired a high degree
of military fame; but which occasioned,
what is little regarded by sovereigns, a miserable effusion of human blood, and was productive of much calamity to the Prussian
dominions, as well as to the neighboring
countries." Another author says, " Frederic, seeing Prussia and Pomerania in the

hands of the Russians, Silesia and Branden-
burg, in considerable part occupied by the
Austrians, and Westphalia by the French ;
finding himself but weakly assisted by his
allies, his army nearly annihilated, no less
through his victories than his defeats, himself
without any money or resources, resolved on
committing an act of suicide in imitation of the
Roman heroes." And he was with difficulty
dissuaded from it by D. Argens, a friend to
whom he had communicated his design. From
this depth of distress he was released by the
death of the Empress of Russia, with whose
successor, Peter 3d, he was (by a singular con-
catenation of circumstances, too intricate to
be here explained,) enabled to make a treaty
of alliance, which was followed by a peace
with Sweden, and soon after by the peace of
Hubertsburg in 1763. Thus terminated the
seven years war. "It was one of the most
sanguinary contests that ever desolated the
globe ; and though the military fame acquired by Frederic was very great, yet it must be
considered a trifling compensation to his subjects for the vast effusion of human blood,
which had been produced by his ambition,
and by that jealousy which his numerous
standing army, and his conduct toward his
neighbors, had naturally and universally in-
spired." Nor was Frederic himself less
jealous of preparations for war in other states.
In 1768, only five years after the peace of
Hubertsburg, every preparation was made
for the sudden renewal of hostilities, and all

his military force was set in motion. General
Nugent, a Scotsman, then Austrian ambassa-
dor at the court of Prussia, fearing for his
mistress the Empress Queen, demanded an
audience and requested to know the intentions of the king.   It turned out that a purchase of 4,000 horses which Maria Theresa
had ordered to reinforce her military establishment, was the cause of all this bustle ;
and on that account Frederic had determined
on making war, and striking the first blow.
Nugent, for whom the king had a great es-
teem, was scarcely able to pacify him, and
succeeded rather by his intimacy as a friend,
than by his diplomacy.   Thus, after so many
calamities, the flame of war was well nigh
lighted up again, by preparation for war ;
and the address and integrity of an individual
were the only means of saving Europe from
desolation.

But England, France, and Prussia are not
the only nations that have brought war on
themselves by military preparations.   In the
table contained in my third number, there
are noticed " 25 wars originating in jealousy
of rival greatness."   My limits do not allow
me to notice any more of them; and I can
barely allude to the present armaments of
Russia, which have roused against her the
jealousy of all the rest of Europe, and may
ere long occasion an extensive and destructive war.

On the other hand, let us contemplate the
conduct of the Quakers, who first settled

Pennsylvania. Though surrounded by tribes
of ferocious savages, they were never attacked ; nor was an individual killed by the Indians ; and no preparation was made for
war. We read of no attack on the Israelites,
when all the males went up to Jerusalem to
worship, from their first establishment in Ca-
naan to the birth of Christ. God, " who has
in his hand the hearts of kings," is as able to
defend peaceable nations now, as he was then :
but "they who take the sword shall perish by
the sword." Though the empire of China is by
no means prepared for war ; and though it
has been asserted that 10,000 European
troops could march through the country, and
that a single frigate could batter down the
fortifications of the Boca Tigris, the strongest in the empire except their useless great
wall ; yet they have long enjoyed peace.
And so great is the emperor's detestation of
war, that he allows no *Christian* missionary
to reside in his dominions ; for he says, " the
christians have whitened with human bones
all the countries into which they have been
admitted." How mortifying is this reproof
of christians from the mouth of a pagan ?
The natives of the Island of Loo Choo, de-
pendant I believe on China, " far surpass the
inhabitants of christian countries in the display of the benignant virtues, and in the art
of preserving peace always among themselves
and with neighboring nations." Travellers
say, " they go perfectly unarmed ; for we saw
no warlike instruments among them of any

description, not even a bow or an arrow was
to be seen,—and the natives always declared
that they had none. They denied any knowledge of war, either by experience or tradi-
tion." It must be evident they had no notions of military glory.

It must be confessed, that though many instances can be adduced to shew that preparations for war produce war ; yet we can on the
other hand adduce but few examples of the
power of pacific principles in preventing it.
For unhappily there are few nations, who do
not pay homage to military prowess, and
idolize their destroyers. The love of glory
causes preparation for war, and preparation
for war reproduces love of glory. Many a
military commander, on reviewing his well
disciplined troops, glittering in arms and
gold, has felt sensations like those ascribed to
Marmion, when he is made to exclaim at
sight of the well ordered Scottish camp—

> ————————"were that host mine,
> Not power infernal nor divine,
> Should once to peace my soul incline,
> Till I had dimmed their armor's shine,
>   In glorious battle fray."

So, to gratify the ambition of despots and
military heroes, hosts of men are driven like
sheep to the slaughter ; and more silly
than sheep, they applaud and idolize their
butchers. Ah ! when will mankind learn,
that the founder of a city is more honorable
than its destroyer ; that a Howard is more
worthy of respect than a Napoleon ; and that
it is more glorious to save than to destroy ?

NO. 14.

The influence of the Female sex often exerted in favor of War.

FEARING I shall exhaust the patience of my readers, I shall mention but one more of the exciting causes of the love of military glory ; and that is *the influence of the Female sex.*

Strange as it may appear, it will be found, on close examination, that the horrors of war, murder, robbery and violation are in part effected by the soft blandishments, the approving smiles, and the fascinating charms of the other sex. Mankind are in every age the same ; and the same chivalrous spirit, which excited the knights of "olden time" to sally forth in quest of perilous adventures, is now excited by the approbation which fashion and beauty lavish on courage, without discrimination of end or object. That "none but the brave deserve the fair," has been so often re-echoed from female lips, that it is regarded as an axiom. But what is bare ferocious courage in the abstract, but a brutal quality, in which the bravest hero that ever drew sword is surpassed by the lion and the rattlesnake, which never flee from danger, and equalled by the dunghill fowl of our barn-yards? Courage is admirable only when it is qualified by virtue ; but when it is united with vice, it becomes execrable. Compare the courage of the soldiers of the cross, who, not only with lion-like fortitude but with dove-like pa-

tience, have serenely borne the torture, the
rack, the flaming fagot, and the red-hot
chain, consuming by slow degrees amid the
taunts and hisses and reproaches and insults
of the surrounding mob; or who have forced,
and are still forcing, their way under the ban-
ners of the cross, into Satan's kingdom, surrounded by death and difficulties and discour-
agements and ingratitude :——Compare the
courage of these men with the so much boasted example of the grenadier, who suffered
himself to be blown up rather than abandon
his post.   In those were true heroism and
greatness of soul, which must be admired so
long as mankind shall regard the rights of
conscience, and the blessings of the gospel.
The other must be regarded as courage, it is
true; but until we are acquainted with the
cause in which it was exerted, we ought to
suspend our approbation.

It is a law of our nature, that persons of
one sex should love those qualities in the other of which they themselves are deficient. As
naturally as the ivy inclines to the oak, and
entwines its weak and slender tendrils round
every branch and twig, so do the soft charms
of the female sex bind our affections with
silken cords, more indissoluble than bands
of adamant, and captivate every power and
affection of our minds. That the weak should
love the strong, and that the strong should
love to protect the weak, is wisely ordered.
That females should honor the man who saves
them from the horrors of war and insults
6

worse than death, is natural and right; but
surely they should detest the wretch, who, for
the sake of gratifying his selfish thirst for
military glory, wantonly subjects them to
such misfortunes. Unhappily they do not
discriminate between the *ability* and the *will*
to do good. Shame on the man, (if he may
be called a man,) who would not venture his
heart's blood to rescue helpless woman; but
many a one would thus willingly venture his
own life, who would not willingly take the
life of others. It is not the warrior exclusively, who would defend the fair sex from
injury. On the contrary, it is certain that
female rights are more in danger from warriors than from all other men. Whether the
story of the British outrages at Hampton be
true or false, the conduct they were charged
with is nothing more than what is common in
war; and if it has not been imitated by our
own soldiers, it is only because they have not
so long followed the trade of war; for there
is no crime, however black, of which war has
not been the parent.

If we examine into the characters of those
military heroes, who have been so much eulogized by the fair, we shall see whether they
have rightly chosen their friends. Of those
I have mentioned in these communications,
Alexander and Frederic were accused of unnatural crimes. The latter, though married,
never cohabited with his wife; and it was
his boast that neither a woman nor a priest
was to be seen in his palace. Charles XII.

was. a brutish woman-hater. Napoleon's
treatment of Josephine in repudiating her and
marrying another, from ambitious motives,
does not shew much regard for the sex;
though he was often surrounded in the public
walks of Paris, by crowds of the most beautiful women in France, who contended for
the honor of embracing his knees. Nor do I
think one of our farmer's wives would like to
exchange her own good man for a Nelson or
a Wellington, did she but know their private
characters, though the ladies of England
have erected a statue to the latter, and if I
remember rightly went into mourning for the
other. As far as I have known the character of military men, they love the sex it is
true; but (with a few honorable exceptions)
only the baser part. They love the sex so
far as they minister to their pleasures, and for
the most part no farther. They pretend to
be their defenders: but against whom do
they defend them? against warriors like
themselves. By making war they bring on
the sex the danger of insult from the lust of
an unbridled soldiery; they butcher their fathers, husbands, lovers and brothers, burn
their houses and destroy their means of sub-
sistence, and pretend they love the sex.
Surely "the tender mercies of the wicked
are cruel."

But it remains to be shewn how the influence of the female sex inflames a love of military glory and thus causes war.

The part which women take in public re-

joicing for victories, has a tendency to this
end. We read in the public papers, during
the late war, that a naval officer, being the
bearer of a captured flag to Washington,
stopped at a town in which at the same moment was a public ball; and that this English ensign was paraded in the ball room,
and that the *ladies* danced round and trampled
on it :—a sight well calculated to inflate the
vanity of the young officer, and fire his
mind with military ardor, make him restless
in peace, desirous for war and willing to
provoke aggression. But this dance resem-
bled that of female savages round the stake,
at which the captive warrior is expiring in
agony, while the belle of the ring plucks the
bleeding eyeball from its socket and puts a
live coal in its place. My fair countrywomen, start not at the comparison; for the
disposition of both these groups is the same
—both rejoice at the misery of others—and
to rejoice at misery and to cause it, is the
same in the eye of omniscience. One act
differs from the other, only as the bright and
polished sword differs from the rusty toma-
hawk; they are the same in substance and
in purpose.

The martial songs, so frequently sung by the
fair, operate on the youthful lover like the
pibrock of the highlander, and inflame him
with an ardent desire to recommend himself
to his Dulcinea by some chivalrous exploit.

Indeed, chivalry is far from being extinct
with us. We hear from time to time of a

military standard being presented by some
"ladie bright," which affords a fine opportunity to display a well turned arm, and—
when in fashion—a slender waist, and to repeat, with great stage effect, the speech
which Papa has written for the occasion. It
also gives to the officer who receives this *favor* a charming opportunity to deliver his *ex-
temporaneous* answer, which if he cannot so
well carry in his head, the circumstances of
the occasion give him a good chance to read
from the inside of his hat, much to the admiration and edification of the surrounding
multitude and to the confusion of the unfortunate newspaper editor who afterwards attempts to make sense or grammar of it. I
never read an account of one of these dis-
plays of modern chivalry, but it reminds me
of the knighting of the famous hero of La
Mancha in the stable yard, where the Lady
Tolosa girded on his sword and the Lady
Miller buckled on his spurs, and sent him
forth with a benediction in quest of perilous
achievements.

But our ladies are not content barely to present the colors. They frequently assemble
at reviews—instead of a tournament—where
they are almost as numerous as the men, and
have the satisfaction of seeing the privates
shoulder firelock with great eclat, while the
general and his aids, mounted on prancing
horses, astonish the fair spectators with a
display of feathers, gold lace. and epaulets,
and cover themselves with dust and glory.
6*

A review or sham fight is the image of " battle and murder and sudden death." In a
woman's mind, the ideas of love and murder
are often associated; but if we should judge
from appearances, we should suppose, that
though the first may often draw her to the
tented field, the latter has frequently the as-
cendancy.   The Roman matrons were present at the gladiatorial shows.   The Spanish
and Portuguese women attend the bull fights,
and the British and American ladies are
fond of sham battles and public executions.

Notwithstanding the mildness of the female sex, and their inclination to sympathy
and pity, not one female writer of any eminence, that I recollect, has ever employed her
pen in favor of peace; though many have
busied themselves in exciting a love of military glory. The most fortunate adventurers
in love, and the most successful seducers,
have been dressed in regimentals; so that
the intrigues of Mars and Venus are not to
be considered barely as a fable of heathen
mythology; and many a coxcomb has assumed the military garb, to favor his designs on
the virtue of the sex. A late writer, who
accompanied an exploring party toward the
Pacific ocean, relates that it is a custom
among some tribes of savages for the females
to excite the males to war. This custom
has its counterpart in civilized society; for
human nature, is every where the same.
But what lady who believes in the truth of
the christian religion, and obeys its peacea-

ble, forbearing and benevolent precepts, can think it becoming to imitate the conduct of the savage?

I think I have shewn that war generally originates in a love of glory, and the applause which infatuated mankind bestow on their destroyers. The remedy is obvious. Let men cease to idolize their oppressors. Let at least a part of the expense, which is now thrown away on military reviews and preparations for war, be expended in enlightening, civilizing and converting the world. Let mankind be more ready to honor their benefactors; to hurl from their pedestals the statues of robbers and murderers, and to place in their room the statues of legislators, agriculturalists, artists, and all who seek the good rather than the destruction of their race. Let the arts of poetry, painting and music cease to be almost exclusively employed in exciting military ambition. Let the female sex distinguish between their benefactors and their oppressors. And finally, let the principles of the religion of the meek and benevolent Jesus prevail on earth, and it will be converted from an Aceldama to a Paradise.

NO. 15.

On the tendency of War to brutalize the mind.

In my last number, I finished the course which I at first proposed, which was to contemplate the causes of war, and propose a remedy. I am aware that much more might have been said to advantage; but my circumstances do not, at present, afford me sufficient leisure, and I fear that my readers would get tired of dry discussion if continued. I propose, in the next place, to point out some of the evils of war, which are in general but little considered, and in fact are always forgotten amid the roar of cannon and the blaze of illuminations and fireworks by which victories are celebrated.

War brutalizes the minds of all who are engaged in it, and renders them ferocious and unpitying.

It is related of the *gallant* Frederic of Prussia, that during the war which he made on the *young queen* of Hungary, when he had the *glory* to wrest from her, almost unresisted, the fair province of Silesia, and thus extend at once his dominions and his *fame*—in this war he one night gave positive orders that every light in his camp should be extinguished by 8 o'clock. The moment the time was passed, he walked to see if all were dark. He found a light in the tent of Capt. Zeitern, which he entered just as that officer was folding up a letter. Zeitern knew him and instantly fell on his knees to entreat his mercy. The king asked him to whom he had been writing. He answered that it was a letter to his wife, in order to finish which, he had retained the candle a few moments. Frederic coolly ordered him to rise and write one line more, which he would dictate.

This line was to inform his wife, without any explanation, that by such an hour the next day, he should be executed. The letter was then sealed, and Frederic himself took charge of having it conveyed, and the next day the Captain was shot.

Thus far the historian;[*] but let us trace the sequel in our imaginations; for though we hear enough more of Frederic, this is the last we hear of Zeitern. On the morrow, amid "the pomp and circumstance of glorious war," behold the victim—shall I say of connubial affection, or of the grim demon of war,—marched amid the ranks of the soldiers of his own regiment to the fatal spot, where the prevost has already arranged the preliminaries. Imagine, if you can, the anguish of his bosom, the theatre of contending passions. His widowed wife, his helpless children, his wounded honor, his disappointed ambition, and the ingratitude of his royal master, by turns distract his mind; and, with a heedless gaze, he views the awful preparations for death. An officer—perhaps his bosom friend, the companion of his dangers and his joys, with whom he has stormed the deadly breach in search of glory—is appointed to give the dreadful command. The file of grenadiers,—perhaps the soldiers of his own company—are ordered to march—halt —dress—make ready—take aim—and——

[*] A sense of truth and justice compels me to state, that the truth of this story is doubted by Thiebault; and it is not even mentioned by Voltaire.

shall I proceed ?   No.   Here let us drop the
curtain, for it is impossible to conceive, much
less describe the horrors of a military execution.   Let us turn our eyes to another scene.
The round moon is rising serenely bright,
over the tall pines, which skirt the tranquil
river Spree, and whose inverted images are
reflected from its glassy bosom.   A light
gleams from the casement of the mansion of
Zeitern, and throws its rays parallel with
those of the moon, which illumine the raft
and the useless sail as they slowly descend
with the current.   The busy hum from the
neighboring village has almost ceased, and

        " drowsy tinklings lull the distant folds."

All is peace around the cottage of Zeitern,
and all is peace within.   The younger children had already said their prayers, in which
their father and their king were not forgotten,
and were laid to sleep.   The eldest son was
sketching the plan of a fortification, and the
daughter was trying a march on the harpsi-
chord.   All was peace in the bosom of the
unconscious widow of Zeitern.   Anon she
hears the post boy's horn.   Her heart palpi-
tates.   Her bosom swells.   She rushes to the
door.   How eagerly she presses the well
known superscription to her lips !   How rav-
enously she devours the wafer, so lately
pressed by the dear lips of her idol !   With
what ecstacy she lifts to heaven her large blue
eyes, beaming with love and glistening with
pious gratitude, as she reads these sentiments

of affection a thousand times repeated, yet
forever new,——Heard ye that shriek ?—Oh!
she sinks, she falls,—take off those frantic
orphans, support their aged grandmother.—
Give air—breathes she ?—No —But mark that
quivering lip : now all again is motionless.
The chill dews stand in thick drops on her
fair marble forehead ; and that eye, through
which so lately shone forth the full effulgence
of love and piety, is now half closed and fixed in glassy listlessness ; and *death* is there.

Daughters of Columbia, suppress the rising
sigh. Drop not a tear on the cold corpse of
the poor broken hearted widow of Zeitern.
Would you tarnish the memory of the *immortal* Frederic ? He has done the duty of a
warrior. No ; were the same times returned, and Frederic yet alive, I should say, hasten to Berlin, and with others of your sex,
shout, " He comes ! he comes, the conqueror
comes !" Shake your white handkerchiefs
in the air ; strew flowers beneath his horse's
feet, kneel and embrace his knees. Let not
the image of Zeitern's orphans cloud your joy.
Let the boys follow the camp, and the girls
too ; or at least let them weep in secret, and
not, by their appearance, mar the triumph of
a glorious victory. Ladies of New England,
does this advice disgust you ? Then thank
him " who hath made you to differ ;" for had
you been born in Berlin, you would have been
ready to act these scenes, when Frederic *the
great* returned from the conquest of Silesia,
which he *gloriously* wrested from the defenceless queen of Hungary.

But should females take no part in such
joyful triumphs of the brave? Take a part?
O, yes, let them take the part for which God
and nature designed them. Let them visit
the cottage of Zeitern and provide for his
helpless orphans and aged mother, and attend to the funeral obsequies of his broken-
hearted widow. Let them visit and console
those who have been bereaved of all earthly
hopes by their country's victories. Let them
visit the prison, where those are confined,
whom the love of glory has made their enemies; bind up their wounds and assuage
their griefs. In such occupations, O how
like ministering angels of mercy they appear.
But on the contrary, if they join the triumph
and the cavalcade, and dance round the captured standard of their fallen enemy, regardless of the anguish, misery and wo attendant
on a victory, they may resemble angels, but
alas! they are the fallen ones.

Has the faint picture, which I have attempted to draw, of the sufferings of the Zeitern family touched the feelings of the reader?—but did not the succeeding battles make
many widows and bereave many parents and
relatives? How is it, that we are affected by
the narration of individual sufferings, more
than by the accounts of the sufferings of thousands or myriads who fall in a battle? It is
not that the fate of each individual is not as
melancholy, and has as many ramifications
of wretchedness, when he falls with thousands, as when he falls alone; but because

the sum of misery, which one glorious victory occasions, is altogether beyond our grasp;
and because the sufferings of individuals are
more easily transferred to our individual feelings. True it is, the fate of a Zeitern, or an
Andre, has something singular in it, and misery is exhibited in a new form. There is
something singular in the ferocity of Frederic, and that unfeeling heart, which could thus
needlessly torture the bosom of an affectionate wife; but stern discipline and a love of
glory demanded the sacrifice. And there was
something still more singular in the tear
which fell from the eye of Washington on
the death warrant of Andre. It is not the
man we blame, but war—and above all, we
execrate that love of glory, which can multiply widows and orphans, and desolate kingdoms, for the selfish and vain pleasure of being called the great. Oh ladies, if you have
ever loved—and what woman has not?—how
can you rejoice when so many widows, who
loved as well as you, are lamenting with bit-
ter tears? How can you rejoice, when so
many mothers, as fond and as doating as
you, are written childless? How can you rejoice, when so many maidens, fair as you,
are lamenting their first love ravished from
them by a fatal victory? How can you rejoice, when you have not only so much cause
to mourn for the victors, but when you think
of the mothers, widows and lovers of the vanquished dead, who never injured you, and
who feel as tenderly as you do? No, veil your

beauties from the sight of man—recede, and weep in secret. It is one thing to be thankful for deliverance from danger, and another to triumph over a fallen enemy. But when you assist at a triumph occasioned by a love of glory, you are accessary to all the murders committed in the victory. You have a fascinating power which binds our sex. We are but what you make us. It is in your power to banish War from the earth, and to restore the empire of Peace. Do you frown on military glory, and that frown annihilates it.

NO. 16.

The means which heroes use to acquire fame.

It may be useful to the cause of peace, to consider the means which great heroes have generally taken, to obtain the applause with which they have been honored.

I send you a few extracts from Thiebault's "Original Anecdotes of Frederic the Great."

"It was the savage William" (viz. Wm. Frederic, father of Frederic the Great, by most writers called Frederic the 2d,) "who established or confirmed the law, making soldiers for their lives of all the lower orders of the Prussians, with few exceptions. When this manner of enlisting was first practised, the distress and consternation it occasioned, was general. Nothing was talked of, but leaving the country. Nothing was more common than to see men cut off one or more of the fingers of their right hand, to be freed at once from the power of the recruiting officer."

Speaking of a review he says, " I cast my eye on a young stripling of fifteen years of age ; and witnessed his taking out of the ranks a soldier, at least fifty, to whom he gave repeated blows with his cane, on his arms and thighs, for some trifling fault he had been guilty of, in the handling of his arms ; while the only reply of the unfortunate sufferer, was silent and indignant tears."

This dreadful severity rendered a great number of soldiers absolutely desperate. "They said each to the other, that the best thing they could do, was to die ; but to prevent their afterwards going to hell, for committing suicide, they would murder some child, (whom by that means they sent to paradise, whither they should then go, of necessity, themselves,) for the purpose of confessing the murder and surrendering their persons : and thus procure themselves the opportunity of asking pardon of God previous to their being condemned to punishment."

" I knew a great number of the soldiery, who had adopted this monstrous doctrine. Frederic conceived against it the most just abhorrence and alarm : and to counteract it, gave strict orders, that no priest or pastor should be allowed to approach a homicide of this description, whose crime, he observed, was more in the spirit of the devil than of re-

ligion. This remedy, at first, produced but
little effect. It was not, however, quite useless. The soldiers could not think, without
utter repugnance, of dying without spiritual
assistance : and feared this privation would,
more infallibly, bring upon them the pains
of damnation."

As it may be supposed, frequent attempts
at desertion and mutiny were made in the army of Frederic, which were generally detected, and punished in the most horrible
manner.

"What renders desertion in Prussia in
time of peace nearly impossible, is the order
established respecting soldiers. Any officer
who sees several soldiers standing together,
may, and ought, to separate them, by blows
with his cane. Every captain, from whose
company a soldier deserts, is put under con-
finement for a limited time. Every garris-
oned town is surrounded by fortifications, by
walls, or at least, by palisades : this inclosure
has within it a periphery, which resembles a
road or place for walking; here the sentinels are so placed as for one to see and hear
another throughout. If a deserter has passed between two of these sentinels, and the
fact is proved, the two sentinels undergo a
flogging. In addition, the muster roll is
called over, three times in the course of every
evening. If there be but one who does not
answer to his name, the strictest search is
immediately made ; and if not found in the
course of an hour, the cannon for alarm is

discharged. This is a cannon of large dimensions, and placed on a high piece of ground, and is heard in all the adjacent villages. This signal assembles the country people, who take up arms, and keep guard at every outlet. A reward of forty livres is paid to any village, that lays hold of a deserter; and, on the other hand, the village, through which a deserter is proved to have passed, is obliged to pay a fine of the same amount."

Frederic employed his officers to kidnap citizens and seduce soldiers, from neighboring states. One of them being detected, the king was informed of it by the proper authorities. He coolly replied, that there was no officer of his army, of that name, who was not at his post. " The captain was therefore led to the scaffold, pronouncing curses on the policy of kings."

Thiebault, who is a professed admirer of Frederic, gives many examples of this kidnapping by the Prussian recruiting parties. Among many others he mentions a German judge, and also a French captain of cavalry, who, accidentally falling in their way, was kidnapped and put into the ranks. The king knew it, but detained him to the end of the war, and then himself coolly dismissed him. A French surgeon shared the same fate, only that he was sooner released, by having friends at court. Indeed it was dangerous for any well made man, of any nation, to travel in or near the Prussian dominions.

In fact, Frederic the Great scrupled not to steal men, in any part of the world, and to keep them in the most abject military slavery ; so that a battle was to them a day of rejoicing as the end of their sufferings.

The conscription under the Great Napoleon was still more universal, than that under the Great Frederic ; though perhaps the discipline was less severe. Napoleon did by persuasion, what Frederic did by punishment; and by permission to plunder and riot and to commit every excess, the timid and simple conscript was, in a few years, converted into a ferocious and blood thirsty soldier.

Every one knows at what a vast sacrifice of liberty and happiness, the naval glory of Great Britain is supported. Who that contemplates her system of impressment but must be astonished, that a nation claiming to be the most free and enlightened of any in Europe, if not in the world, should tolerate so great an infringement on the liberty of the subject. But if ever my countrymen shall be as much infatuated by the glare of military and naval glory, as the French and English, they will as tamely submit to conscription and impressment. War knows no rights, but the rights of the strongest. Its maxim is, " the end justifies the means." And it is by means such as I have narrated, that all military heroes, with but few exceptions, have acquired their renown. As well may we expect to have slavery without scourges and gags and fetters, as military glory without conscriptions and impressments, and the most abject servitude of common sailors and soldiers. Who that loves liberty, can love war ? How can the same person worship Liberty, and adore tyrants ?

NO. 17.

State of the wounded after the battle of Waterloo.

THE horrors of war, when seen from a distance, or seen through the medium of the senses of others, are but little regarded; and if, occasionally, they are presented to our imagination, the shouts of victory, the pomp of triumph, the cavalcade, the music, and the roaring cannon, drive them from the minds of the victors; while envy, malice and revenge take possession of the thoughts of the vanquished. It is impossible to draw a correct picture of the horrors of a battle ; but I have been somewhat affected by a faint and partial outline of the scenes which succeeded the *glorious* victory of Waterloo. It was drawn incidentally by Mr. Charles Bell, surgeon of the Middlesex hospital, London, who followed the army for the sake of perfecting himself in the knowledge of gunshot wounds and enriching his celebrated lectures on surgery. He says,

"Before I arrived at Brussels, the battle of Waterloo had been fought. ****** I had been for some days engaged in making my notes and sketches, in the public hospitals, when report led me to an empty barrack, afterwards called the Hospital de la Gendarmeric. Here the very worst aspect of war presented itself : our soldiers were bringing in the French wounded. They continued to be brought in for *several successive days;* and I saw the British soldiers, who in the morning were moved by the piteous cries of those they carried, in the evening, hardened by the repetition of the scene, and by fatigue, and indifferent to the sufferings they occasioned."

" It was now the *thirteenth day after the battle.* It is impossible for the imagination to conceive the sufferings of men, rudely carried at such a period of their wounds. When I first entered this hospital, these Frenchmen had been roused and excited, in an extraordinary degree ; and in the glance of their eyes there was a character of fierceness, which I never thought to have witnessed in the human countenance. They were past the utterance of what, if I might read the countenance, was unsubdued hatred and desire of revenge."

" On the second day the temporary excitement had subsided. Turn which way I might, I encountered every form of entreaty from those, whose condition left no need of words, to stir compassion. " *Surgeon Major, oh, how I suffer ! Dress my wounds, dress my wounds !—Doctor, I commend myself to you ; cut off my leg. Oh ! I suffer too much, too much.*" And when these entreaties were unavailing, you might hear in a weak inward voice of despair, "*I shall die; I am a dead man.*" The tones were too true to nature, soon to lose their influence. At four in the morning, I offered my services: and at six I entered on the most painful duty of my life, in inspecting and operating these unfortunate men. I was thus engaged uninterruptedly, from six in the morning till seven at night, for three successive days." *****

"I know not what notions my feeling countrymen have of thirty thousand (wounded) men, thrown into a town and its environs. They still their compassionate emotions by subscriptions: but what avails this to the wounded, who would exchange gold for a bit of rag. If men would encounter the painful reality, and allow themselves for a moment to think of the confusion that must attend such a scene; the many, very many cases, where knowledge, decision and dexterity are more necessary, than in any other situation in life. If they would consider, that from the pressure of time, the surgeon requires personal and constitutional strength, as well as the promptitude gained by long study and experience, they would be led to inquire, what duties had been performed, and what considerations had attended the unexampled exertions of the army surgeons, after the battle of Waterloo."

These concluding sentences are the reflections of a surgeon, and a humane one too: but what must be the feelings of a philanthropist, on viewing so horrible a scene!

My heart sickens at the contemplation, and
I am obliged to turn away from this picture
of human misery, caused by pride, ambition,
a love of military glory, and the folly of
mankind in paying adoration to their destroyers. Would not angels weep at such a
scene as this? But is this all? Ah no.
Each of these dead or wounded soldiers had
a mother, who had dandled him on her
knees, and watched over his cradle, and had
attended him in his sickness, and shed over
him the tears of maternal solicitude. Each
had a father, who had labored for his support, and reared his youth to manhood, in
the fond expectation, that in old age, he
should reap the reward of his paternal anxi-
ety. Many had wives and lovers, to whom
they were dearer than the light of the sun.
Many had children who looked to them for
support and protection. We may rationally
suppose that for every man who was killed
or wounded, in this deadly conflict, the
hearts of at least ten parents, wives, children,
brothers and sisters were lacerated. Oh what
hecatombs of sacrifices on the bloody altar
of Moloch! How long will mankind continue to be accessary to such crimes, by be-
stowing praises on their perpetrators? How
long will it be, ere every human being will
deem it his imperious and solemn duty to
disseminate the principles of Peace, and extend her empire?

NO. 18.

The influence of the Christian Religion to alleviate the horrors of War.

WHEN we look back on the manner in which war was carried on in ancient times, and compare the cruelties then exercised on the vanquished, with the treatment of prisoners since the promulgation of the Christian religion—or when we compare the manner in which wars are now prosecuted by Pagans and Mahometans with the more mild, yet still horrible, hostilities of christian nations—when we reflect on the black hole of Calcutta and the murders of Scio, we are constrained to allow that the Christian religion —though more professed than practised—has done much to alleviate the calamities of war. Yet alas! how few, " that name the name of Christ," are " careful to depart from *all* iniquity." But we find that as the glorious light of the blessed gospel of peace is more widely and more generally diffused, the evils of war are diminished. Perhaps at no time since the apostolic age has pure and undefiled religion so generally prevailed, as at the present; nor has peace among christian nations been so general. There is scarce a " speck of war" in the horizon. There has been a very evident change in public opinion respecting war. And we have great reason to hope that the time is not far distant, when men " shall beat their swords into plough-

shares and their spears into pruning hooks,
and nation shall not lift up sword against nation, neither shall they learn war any more.'

I have been led to these reflections by
reading the President's last message. I do
not know any thing of late that has so much
rejoiced my heart. I refer particularly to
the section relating to privateering ; and as
many of your readers, particularly females,
are not fond of reading long documents,
and may not have read this section, I insert
it.

"At the commencement of the recent war
between France and Spain, it was declared
by the French government, that it would
grant no commissions to privateers, and that
neither the commerce of Spain herself, nor
of neutral nations, should be molested by the
naval force of France, except in the breach
of a lawful blockade. This declaration,
which appears to have been faithfully carried
into effect, concurring with the principles
proclaimed and cherished by the United
States, from the first establishment of their
independence, suggested the hope that the
time had arrived when the proposal for adopting it as a permanent and invariable rule in
all future maritime wars, might meet the favorable consideration of the great European
powers. Instructions have accordingly been
given to our ministers with France, Russia
and Great Britain, to make those proposals
to their respective governments. And when
the friends of humanity reflect on the essen-

tial amelioration to the condition of the human race, which would result from the abolition of private war on the sea, and on the great facility by which it might be accomplished, requiring only the consent of a few sovereigns, an earnest hope is indulged that these overtures will meet with an attention, animated by the spirit in which they were made, and that they will ultimately be successful."

Yes Sir, I think that the United States' being the first nation in the world to propose the abolition of *private war on the ocean*, reflects on their history more true and lasting glory than the battles of Bunker's Hill and New-Orleans. But I should be glad to see our worthy chief magistrate go one step further, and propose the abolition of *public war on the land*. "And when the friends of humanity reflect on the essential amelioration to the condition of the human race, which would result from the abolition of the" custom of war, " and the great facility by which it might be accomplished, requiring only the consent of" the people, " an earnest hope is indulged" that the efforts of the friends of Peace will be successful—that mankind will at length open their eyes to their true interests, and cease to be dazzled by the *ignis fatuus* of military glory, or to be led blindfold to their destruction by blood-thirsty tyrants.

But while we should rejoice at the extermination or rather the reformation of priva-

8

teersmen, bucaniers and pirates, it becomes
us to inquire in what they differ from other
warriors, except in the magnitude of the evils
they inflict.   This reminds me of the regula-
tions of the race course near Charleston, S.
C. which prohibit hustle—cap, chuck far-
thing, and the wheel of fortune, by which the
boys lose their cents, while they encourage
the greater gambling of the course, by which
whole plantations are squandered, and many
a poor negro is brought to the hammer.   It
is taking "tythes of mint, anise and cummin,"
while the weightier matters of the law are
neglected.   This they ought to do, and not
leave the other undone.

NO. 19.

Buonaparte's Peninsular War.

IT is one of the evils of war, that victory
gilds the blackest of characters, and that
crimes, which in private individuals would
meet their merited detestation, either pass
unnoticed when committed by conquerors,
or are palliated on the score of necessity—
the Devil's plea—necessity !—yes, they are
necessary to conquest, subjugation and slavery, and therefore excusable !

I have been led to these reflections by some
late panegyrics I have read on the character
and conduct of Buonaparte, and a review of
Southey's History of the Peninsular War.
But it is out of the power of Las Cases and
O'Meara to gild a character, which appears

the blacker the more it is examined, and
which must descend to posterity, associated
with Nero's and Caligula's. Though the re-
straints of the age in which he lived, prevented him sometimes from acting out, and at
other times forced him to conceal, his intentions; and his greater talents enabled him to
be more greatly wicked and more *gloriously*
mischievous. It must be allowed that there
are here and there some light spots in his
character, which shine like a few twinkling
stars in a vast expanse of blackness ; on
which alone his admirers would fix the eye
of the spectator, and draw it away from the
vast surrounding darkness.

It would far exceed my greatest limits,
were I to detail the bribery, falsehood and
perfidy, by which Napoleon the great, with
the assistance of the infamous Godoy—at
once the paramour of the Queen and the con-
fidant of the King—made prisoners of the
whole royal family of Spain—drew off the
flower of the Spanish armies to fight his battles of the north of Europe—got possession
of the fortresses, castles and military posts—
and placed his puppet brother on the throne,
thus gratifying his arrogant and vain-glorious
lust of universal dominion.

The train of perfidy, whereby Buonaparte
had thus far accomplished his purpose, is unexampled even in the worst ages of history.
The whole transaction was a business of pure,
unmingled treachery, unprovoked, unextenu-
ated; equally detestable in its motives, its
means, and its end !

"But the hour of retribution was at hand."
The Spaniards soon found to their cost that
they had exchanged a *log* for a *cormorant ;*
and mean and servile as they are commonly
esteemed—rose in one universal bust of indignation. The contest commenced at Madrid—but what could an unarmed multitude
effect against the myrmidons of Napoleon,
inured to victory and crimes ? The people
when they felt the superiority of the French,
fled into the houses. The doors were broken
open, and all within, who were found with
arms, were bayonetted, and parties of cavalry were stationed at the different outlets of
Madrid, to pursue and cut down those who
were flying from the town." The slaughter
among the Spaniards had been very great ;
this, however, did not satisfy Murat ; con-
formably to the system of his master, the
work of death was to be continued in cool
blood. A military tribunal, under General
Grouchy, was formed ; and the Spaniards
who were brought before it, were sent away
to be slaughtered, with little inquiry whether
they had taken any part in the struggle, or
not. Three groups of forty each, were suc-
cessively shot in the Prado. Others in like
manner were put to death in different parts
of the city. " In this manner was the evening of the second of May employed by the
French at Madrid. The inhabitants were
ordered to illuminate their houses, ***** and
through the whole night the dead and dying
might be seen distinctly as in broad day, ly-

ing upon the bloody pavement. When morning came, the same mockery of justice was continued, and fresh murders were committed, deliberately, with the forms of military execution, during several succeeding days."

We are obliged to pass over the disgusting and thrilling detail of atrocities committed by the French invaders; but we are compelled to stop a moment at the seige of Zaragoza; where the war was waged with so diabolical a spirit, that it would seem as if Napoleon had drawn on his allies of the lower regions, for recruits to fill up the ranks of his army.

" It was on the morning of the 15th of June, that the French troops advanced to the first assault of the city *** The patriots lost 4000 men in killed and wounded, and the carnage among the French was yet more frightful ***. On the 27th, the enemy, now re-inforced by several thousands of fresh troops, attacked the city and the Torrero [an adjacent height] but were in both quarters repulsed with the loss of 800 men. On the following morning, they renewed both assaults; from the city they were again driven, but of the Torrero they gained possession; and their train of mortars and other artillery having arrived, commenced from thence an incessant and most destructive fire of shot and shells on the city. Amidst this dreadful scene, some wretches, whom the French had found means to corrupt, fired the great powder magazine and destroyed 200 lives, and a furious assault immediately commenced.

8*

But both this and frequent repetitions of it
were successfully resisted.

" On the 4th of August, the French open-
ed their batteries, within pistol shot of the
church and convent of St. Eugracia. The
mud walls [of the city] were levelled at the
first discharge ; and the besiegers, rushing
through the opening, took the batteries before
the adjacent gates in reverse. The convent
of St. Francisco and the general hospital
were stormed and set on fire. The sick and
wounded threw themselves from the windows
to escape the flames, and the horror of the
scene was aggravated by the maniacs, whose
voices raving or singing in paroxysms of
wilder madness, or crying to be set free, were
heard amid the confusion of dreadful sounds.
Many fell victims to the fire, and some to the
indiscriminating fury of the assailants. After a severe contest and dreadful carnage, [in
which the women and children must be necessarily involved,] the French forced their
way into the Cezo, in the very centre of the
city ; and before the day closed, were in possession of one half of Zaragoza. The contest, which was now carried on, is unexampled in history." One side of the street was
possessed by the French, and the other by
the Spaniards. " The intervening space was
presently heaped with dead, either slain upon
the spot, or thrown out of the windows. The
next day the ammunition of the citizens began to fail. It was almost death to appear
by daylight within reach of those houses

which were occupied by the other party; but
under cover of night, the combatants frequently dashed across the street to attack
each other's batteries, and the battles which
began there were often carried on into the
houses beyond, where they fought from room
to room, and floor to floor.—A new horror
was added to the dreadful circumstances of
war ***. In general engagements, the dead
are left upon the field of battle, and the sur-
vivors remove to clear ground, and untainted
atmosphere ; but here,—in Spain, in the
month of August, where the dead lay, the
struggle was still carried on, and pestilence
was dreaded from the enormous accumulation
of putrifying bodies ***. The only remedy was
to tie ropes to the French prisoners, and push
them forward, amid the dead and dying, to
remove the bodies and bring them away for
interment. Even for this necessary office
there was no truce, and it would have been
certain death to the Aragonese, who should
have attempted to perform it."

At length the French were expelled from
the city, but the French generals throughout
Spain "invariably" permitted their troops
"to pillage and commit the most horrible
atrocities on the inhabitants."

But "whatever oppressions the French
exercised in other countries : whatever enor-
mities they committed in Spain, were mercy and humanity in comparison with their
conduct in Portugal. Even while the inhabitants remained in unresisting obedience,

there were no bounds to the extortions and
robberies and insolence of their task masters.
The most respectable and opulent families
were reduced to beggary, by the enormous
amount of forced loans and contributions
imposed on them : the peasantry were so
overcome by despair, as to neglect putting
seed into the ground. The churches were
sacrilegiously robbed of their ornaments and
plate : the troops universally lived at free
quarters on the inhabitants, and plundered
their houses of money and clothing: and
while the horror-stricken and indigent people
saw the sanctuaries of their religion defiled,
the arms of their monarchy defaced, and a
French military government avowedly established on the ruins of their independence,
the insults of their brutal oppressors were
carried to the very bosom of their families;
prostitutes were forced into their society, and
happy was the man who preserved his wife
and daughter from contagion, and worse than
contagion. But when the provinces, inspir-
ed by the example of Spain, about June,
1808, rose in insurrection, the monsters,
whose tyranny had maddened the people into
resistance, made it the signal and the excuse
for the indulgence of every devilish passion.
The detachments ordered by Junot under
Loison and others, to chastise the country,
perpetrated barbarities, which would be here-
after incredible, if our eyes had not seen
them, and if contemporary historians had
not betrayed them.—Prisoners butchered;

females first violated and then murdered;
towns sacked and burned to ashes; men,
women and children indiscriminately murdered in cold blood.—These were the often
repeated scenes, which terminated only when
Junot * * was obliged * * to recall his ferocious and murderous bands to Lisbon, to oppose the landing of the destined liberators of
this wretched people."

Now what was the first moving cause of all
this treachery, murder and rapine? Ambition.
Napoleon must have dominion and glory,
and infatuated mortals are ready to give
them to him; and because he has been vic-
torious, to bury all his crimes in oblivion, or
to extenuate, and even to admire them. If
war was ever justifiable on either side, surely the inhabitants of the Peninsula must be
justified in fighting for their hearths and al-
tars; but how little compassion is shown
them by many citizens of this *enlightened*
country! and while they are deaf to the cries
of the violated female, the distracted mother,
and the expiring infant, they feel a sickly
compassion for the author of all their wrongs,
because, for the peace and security of the
world, he was confined on a distant island,
with all the luxuries which art could furnish,
and at an expense exceeding the salaries of
our Executive and all the heads of depart-
ments. I do not wish, in the least, to excul-
pate the infamous conduct of the self-styled
Holy Alliance! and as a republican, a man,
and a christian, I cannot view their conduct,

without abhorrence ; and think them guilty
of murder for every death they have occasioned in Spain.—But I cannot help thinking
it strange, that many, who are vehement in
their execration of the authors of the late war
in Spain, endeavor to screen Napoleon from
the public execration, which he has justly
merited, instead of calling on Heaven for
tenfold vengeance to blast,—but no, I would
not curse him. He has gone to render up an
account of his deeds, and must indeed be an
object of pity, if he has to endure one thou-
sandth part of the misery he has caused to
others. My heart may bleed for him ; but I
dare not, in the face of heaven, extenuate his
crimes. No, I would not curse him ; and to
me it would have-afforded the most heart-felt
satisfaction, to have perceived the least ray
of hope that he had, at the last moment of
his earthly existence, found mercy through
the blood of the Lamb, who was slain to
atone for his sins and mine.

NO. 20.

The expenses of War.

One of the evils of war, though of minor
importance, is the *immense expense.*

"It appears, from the statistical tables, in
Lowe's present state of England, that the wars
which grew out of the French revolution,
commencing in 1793, and ending in 1815, cost
Great Britain eleven hundred millions of
pounds sterling." Reckoning after the com-

mon (though erroneous) method of comput-
ing the pound sterling at $4,44, the sum
would amount to 4,884 millions of dollars, or
at the current exchange to more than five
thousand millions of dollars. This amount
is altogether beyond our conception. Nor is
it worth the time, to calculate how many tons
of silver it would amount to, how many ships
it would load, how many acres it would cover, how many times it would encompass the
earth, or how many centuries it would take a
man to count it ;—the amount would still exceed the imagination. For our ideas of numbers, whether applied to dollars or to murders, affect us, more by the contiguity of the
subjects to which they are applied, than by
their magnitude. One murder in our own
family affects us more than the many thousands, perpetrated in the Russian campaign ;
and a dollar, taken from our own pockets, is
more regarded by us than the whole national
debt of Great Britain. The very interest of
the above named sum, at 5 per cent, amounts
to 250 millions of dollars. In 1808 the population of Great Britain and Ireland was
13,962,070. Reckoning it now at fifteen millions, the average would be $16,66 & 2-3 to
each man woman and child. As the national
debt far exceeds the amount of five thousand
millions of dollars, and might have been reduced so much, had not the war with France
taken place, it follows that that war has en-
tailed on posterity the above named annual
tax of $16,66 & 2-3 for each individual of

the nation, or $83,33 for each family of five
persons,—that it cuts off the comforts and almost the necessaries of the laboring classes;
and disables a poor man from maintaining a
family, without assistance from the parish, so
that it is almost a rule, for the most healthy
and laborious, to apply for such assistance, as
soon as they have two children. This increases the poor rates to an average of nearly
half the income of the rich,—for what the poor
cannot pay the rich must. I have heard an
intelligent banker in London say, that his
taxes amounted to half his income, and that
some reckoned them at even seventeen shil-
lings in the pound. So that the poor, notwithstanding their integrity and industry, go
supperless to bed, and the rich are deprived
of half their income, solely on account of
this one war. Surely this is paying dearly
for glory.

On the continent of Europe it is still worse.
If the national debts do not amount to so
much, as in Great Britain, it is because the
governments have not the credit to obtain
loans, and the people are too poor to lend.
But " in peace they prepare for war" by
wringing every doit they can obtain from the
people, which is hoarded up in their treasu-
ries, and thus the country is drained of spe-
cie. Frederic the great, called by his con-
temporaries "the highwayman of the North,"
used to have the silver and gold manufactured
into picture frames, balustrades, furniture,
&c. which when wanted for military pur-

poses were coined into money. In time of war the continental sovereigns practise conscription in one form or another, and thus save both bounty and wages. I do not know, what is now the pay of a Russian soldier; but, during the last war, if I remember rightly, it was five copecks a day, which, at the exchange of 20 cents per rouble, (and it has been less,) would be but a cent a day; and his allowance, sour, black bread, made of unsifted rye and barley meal, with a modicum of salt, but no meat. The soldiers and most of the inhabitants of the continent fare but little if any better, for which they may thank the warlike spirit of their rulers. And when my countrymen wish for the same *blessings*, they have only to encourage a military spirit; and they will be successful.

To bring the matter nearer home, let us consider a little, the expenses of the last war. Some have computed the *actual expense* at two hundred millions of dollars, and that the loss of trade, navigation, fisheries, &c. amounted to as much more. Lest that calculation should appear extravagant, we will take but one quarter of it; for the expenses of war, like the distance of the fixed stars, are so far beyond our conception, that a few millions or hundreds of millions, added to, or subtracted from the amount, make no sensible difference. Let us consider what that hundred millions of dollars would have procured for us. It would make one hundred thousand miles of turnpike roads, and would

be sufficient to bring a good road to every
man's door; build bridges over rivers, where
they were necessary; and the balance would
raise a fund for keeping both roads and
bridges in perpetual repair without any road
tax; but on the contrary, a great sum of
ready money would be laid out every year
among the farmers, for keeping the roads in
repair. It would make twenty such canals
as the Grand Canal of New York. It would
lock every considerable river in the United
States, and dig canals in every direction
where the tolls would keep them in repair,
and thus double the value of the products of
the interior; bring lumber and other heavy
articles to market at a small expense, and
quadruplicate the value of lands; and the excess of the tolls would pay all the *peace* expenses of government. The interest would
support 20,000 school masters at three hundred dollars a year, which is one for every
five hundred inhabitants; or ten thousand
ministers at six hundred dollars, which is
equal to one for every thousand. Now what
have we got for our money in lieu of all
these benefits? We have got glory—that is
in our own estimation, for the English no
more allow that we beat them, than we allow that they beat us—and triumphantly ask,
what point of the controversy they surren-
dered, and whether we did not leave our disputes and differences with them in the *statu
quo ante bellum?* as is the case in most wars.
So that the greater part of our glory, must
remain for home consumption.

But is there no other glory than military glory? Yes, there is a glory, even of a temporal nature, as far before it, as food is preferable to poison:—De Witt Clinton, Jacob Perkins and Robert Fulton, though I could name many others, have conferred more honor on their country, than all the generals and commodores of the war. The genius that planned the Grand Canal, and the enterprise which undertook, and the energy which accomplished that stupendous work, have astonished the old world. Perkins has shewn to Europe, that the human race is not "belittled" in America; and Fulton, (would we could forget his topedoes,) has shewn a new application of the irresistible force of steam, which has added to the comfort, the convenience, and the wealth of the civilized world. These are the men who have raised the name of their country abroad, altered the tone of the British reviewers, brought forth such floods of compliments from our former revilers, and covered this country with a glory as far superior to military fame, as the unfailing, animating and invigorating light of the sun is superior to the flash of lightning, which dazzles while it blasts us. But glory is a small part, or rather no part, of the utility of the wonders performed by our illustrious fellow citizens. They will continue to be useful and to be admired, for centuries to come, perhaps as long as the sun and moon shall endure;—unless a state of war and vandalism should return, and

they should fall its victims, and suffer the
same fate as the arts of the ancients and the
canals of Egypt—which, indeed, is as un-
likely as another deluge; for the christian
religion, like God's bow in the Heavens, is a
sure pledge that such a flood of war and barbarism, shall never again inundate the world.
Not so with military glory. It is driven
away like chaff before the wind. What is
the glory of the Scipios and the Cæsars to
the present inhabitants of Rome? Yet they
continue to slake their thirst by the aque-
ducts and fountains provided by the ancients,
and are charmed by the verses of their poets
and the eloquence of their orators; and the
Roman roads are still used as highways, not
only in the neighborhood of Rome, but in remote parts of Europe.

I have already exceeded my proposed limits, and must leave many topics on this subject untouched; but I cannot refrain from
two observations more.

The enemies of missions often inveigh
against the expense of them, and pretend to
fear that it will impoverish the country. But
it is, I believe, an undoubted fact, that the expense of maintaining one ship of the line, in
actual service, exceeds the whole expense, not
only of our missionary stations, but also of
all our public benefactions of a religious nature.

A French gentleman of my acquaintance
was present, when we got the first news of the
declaration of the last war : he lifted up his

eyes and hands to Heaven, and exclaimed, "My God! this country tire for being happy." He had been a conscript, and had known something of the horrors of war, of which he said we were ignorant. I never hear of a free and prosperous country involving itself in war, but I mentally exclaim with the Frenchman, this country is tired of being happy.

NO: 21.

The prostration of liberty attendant on a state of Warfare.

I purpose to mention, for the present, but one more of the evil effects of war; for should I continue to enumerate them, and to point out all the barbarity, cruelty, slavery, iniquity and sin attendant on a state of war, the age of man, and the *pen of an angel* would not suffice.

I would now call the attention of my readers, to the entire prostration of liberty attendant on a state of war, and the horrible punishments inflicted on the instruments of it.

War often makes it *necessary* to suspend the writ of habeas corpus and the trial by jury; and civilians and even divines are liable to be dragged before a military tribunal, or to be imprisoned, flogged and executed. The general is often sole judge of this necessity—and military men seldom neglect an opportunity to lord it over the characters of civil life, for whom they have, commonly, an utter con-

9*

tempt ; and martial law is often proclaimed
barely for the purpose of extending the power of the commander, and gratifying his arrogant love of dominion. It is wonderful,
that the chief who most frequently breaks
over the limits of the constitution, tramples
on the laws and infringes on the liberty of
his fellow citizens,—if only successful in attacking an enemy, or repelling an invasion—
is hailed as the savior of his country, and receives all the honors, which that country can
confer ;—as though territory were dearer to
us than our liberties. Public opinion needs
correction in this particular :—for territory
lost may be recovered, but liberty once lost,
is lost forever.   No country in the world was
ever free but once—except that a subdued
people have sometimes thrown off a *foreign*
yoke—but the country which has suffered itself to be enslaved by *its own* soldiers, if ever
it has recovered its liberty, the relief has been
only temporary and succeeded by a harder
servitude.   The nation, therefore, which
voluntarily engages in war, hazards the irre-
trievable loss of the greatest temporal blessing which God has bestowed on man.

But the instruments of war are themselves
the most unhappy victims of its cruelties.
Almost all the governments, on the continent
of Europe, practise conscription in some
form or other. In Prussia every person capable of bearing arms, is compelled, when
called on, to be a soldier, and liable to be
marched from home at the will of the king,

who sends out his officers to take whom they
please. We have no idea of the horrors of
conscription in this country. What inducement has a father to give his son an education, or a trade, where he is every moment,
liable to be dragged into the ranks, and made
a slave for life, and "food for powder"? But
this is *necessary* in military countries; and
had our last war continued two years longer,
it would have been necessary in this. Habit,
however, reconciles people at last, to such
calamities. The poor negro, over-worked
and half starved, becomes at length partially
reconciled to his lot, if he sees that the ne-
groes of the neighboring plantations are no
better off; and if his situation is superior to
others, he almost forgets that he is a slave. I
shall leave it to the moralists and metaphysi-
cians to decide, whether insensibility to misery takes away its sting or only blunts it. We,
thank Heaven, are now free and happy. God
forbid that we should be obliged to appreciate
our privileges by the loss of them.

In England, and in this country, it is true,
there is, as yet, no conscription. But how
much better is the rendezvous? There liquors
are provided for every one who will drink.
Many sober, industrious heads of families are
induced to sip the circean draught, until their
habits are corrupted, and they become fit only for the camp. Our naval rendezvous are
no better, but generally worse.

In England the servile and barbarous custom of impressment prevails, and meets the

general detestation of good men on both sides
of the *Atlantic ;* and, like the above mentioned practices, is only tolerated on the score of
necessity. How absurd and how wicked to
encourage the custom of war, which makes
so many abominations *necessary !* While we
bless ourselves that we have not yet witnessed conscription and impressment; let us remember with alarm, that both were seriously
proposed in congress during the last war, and
had the war continued, both would have been
found *necessary.*

Nor are these violent methods of obtaining
soldiers confined to Christians. Mahomedans
and Pagans are no better. Wherever the
custom of war prevails, there slavery is imposed on the weak by the strong,—on the
foolish by the cunning,—and we may add,
on the virtuous by the vicious. Messrs. Fisk
and King, in their journal in Egypt, say,
" Near Shobreh we met a crowd in the street,
composed principally of women and children,
following some soldiers, who were leading
along a number of Arabs with their hands
bound. The women were weeping, and
shrieking, and crying " my liver ! my liver !"
We found that the young men had been pressed, as soldiers, by order of government."
Here is an Egyptian picture of French conscription and English impressment. Surely,
these Turks are almost as bad as Christians,
—but not altogether, for they follow the dic-
tates of their bloody religion, while Christians
act in direct opposition to the religion they
profess to believe.

When the French General Moreau was in this country, he observed, that we should not go to war, for, we had no *materials* out of which to form an army. Whether the General meant this as a compliment or a reproach, I am uncertain,—but from what I have ever heard or seen of him, I believe he was a friend to the country. In whatever way we take his remark it is however true, and God grant it may always remain so. The difficulty of obtaining soldiers and sailors in the last war, was very great, and enormous bounties were offered in vain. But had we been a warlike nation, this difficulty would not have been so much felt, for war not only reproduces itself, but also manufactures its own materials; and a long continuance of the war would have produced *vice* and *poverty* enough to have filled the ranks, or have given to government the power to do it by force.

I had intended to condense my ideas on this topic into one number, but I find the subject grows so much under my pen, that I am constrained to put off the evils and miseries suffered by soldiers and sailors in actual service, to my next number.

NO. 22.

On the cruelty and degradation to which privates in the navy and army are subject.

IN my last number, I considered the effect of war on personal liberty, as far as it re-

spects the nefarious methods made use of to
procure soldiers and sailors—but the misery
of the soldier and sailor does not end with
trepanning, conscription and impressment.
These are only " the beginning of sorrows."
Nor are the camp fever, wounds and death,
all the evils they have to endure. It is *necessary* to keep them in a state of discipline, in
comparison to which the servitude of a whip-
galled slave, on a rice plantation, is freedom
itself. I have heard the captain of a British
man-of-war order a man to the gangway, to
receive a dozen lashes, for having on *blue*
trowsers. The imprecations and curses heaped on the sailors every time they are ordered
to any duty, is at once degrading to him who
uses such epithets, and to him to whom they
are applied. I do not say that this custom is
general or even common ; but to this degradation, as well as the boatswain's cat-o'-nine-
tails, sailors are subject every moment of
their lives, and the least complaint brings
them to the gangway. It is not uncommon
to sentence sailors to receive five hundred to
a thousand lashes; which are inflicted day
after day, as he is able to bear them. He is
attended at each whipping by a surgeon, who
is to judge how great pain he can bear, without immediate danger to life ; and the flagel-
lation often proceeds until the victim faints,
and then he is respited, to renew his sufferings, on another day. This account I had
from a British surgeon. I have often shud-
dered, and my flesh has crawled, at the reci-

tal of whippings through the fleet, keel-haul-
ing, the spread eagle, gagging, hand-cuffing,
and other punishments inflicted on sailors,
who have been trepanned or impressed into
a service, from which all escape is hopeless,
and death is the only release. This may be
all *necessary*, but how abominable is the custom of war, which *makes* it necessary! And
how atrocious is the practice of impressment,
which subjects men to cruelties, ten-fold
worse than death, inflicted by the will and
caprice of others, without any benefit of a
jury, or hope of redress! Yet a navy is *necessary* to war, and impressment is *necessary*
to a navy; and those who advocate war,
must, at the same time, justify impressment,
cruelty and slavery.

Nor is the condition of soldiers better
than that of sailors; but rather worse. I
was once in the Isle of Wight, where were
stationed some German regiments, in British pay. It was necessary to put them on
an island, to prevent desertions; which, however, were frequent; and the deserter, when
taken, was generally punished by the *gaunt-
lope*. I was on parade, one day, when preparation was making for that kind of punishment. All the soldiers of the regiment,
consisting of six hundred or more, were placed in two ranks, facing each other, and
about five feet apart. To each soldier was
given a stick of a yard in length or more. I
did not stay to see the execution, for I
thought the pain, I must necessarily endure

in witnessing it, would not be compensated
by the gratification of my curiosity. I consequently left the ground before the punishment began. I was however informed that
the culprit was stripped naked to the waist,
with his hands tied before him, and marched
between the ranks, preceded by a drum, and
a soldier walking backwards, with his bayonet presented to the sufferer's breast, to prevent him from going too fast. In this way,
he was struck once by each soldier, officers
going down on the outside of the ranks, to
see that each man does his duty; and if any
one is *suspected* of not laying on hard enough,
he receives, himself, a blow from the officer's
cane. Sometimes the deserter has to retrace
his steps, and as a regiment consists of from
six hundred to a thousand, and some German regiments even of two thousand, he
must, on such an occasion, receive from
twelve hundred to two thousand, and even
four thousand blows, which often proves fatal. To so high a pitch of despair were these
soldiers carried by their sufferings, that many
committed suicide, and one man shot himself
near to my lodgings.

I have seen, on the Continent, the dreadful instrument of torture, called the *picket*,
and as the turf was worn away around it, it
was probably much used. A picket is a stake
standing about a foot out of the ground, and
sharpened to about the size of an English
sixpence. A pole, a rod long, acting on a
pivot, is supported by a neighboring wall, or

a crutch like a well pole, and similar to that
used for tying up slaves to be flogged, in the
southern states. One hand of the sufferer is
made fast to this pole, by a noose round the
wrist, and the other end is depressed, by
which he is elevated from the ground, so
that he can scarcely touch it. Sometimes
an upright post, with a pully, by which the
soldier is hoisted by the wrist, is used instead
of the well pole. He has no alternative but
to *rest* his bare foot on the sharp point of the
stake, or to hang by one arm, with the noose
tightening round the wrist.

The *wooden horse* I have never seen, as it
has been for some time, I believe, discontinued, *because it often ruptured the soldiers, and
rendered them unfit for duty*. It consisted of
a rail, or sharp plank, or two boards nailed
together, at a sharp angle, supported by
posts, six or seven feet high, placed on
trucks, so as to be trundled round the camp.
On this *horse, infantry* soldiers were made to
ride, with their hands tied behind them, and
muskets tied to their feet, as it was *jocularly*
said, to keep their horse from throwing
them.

Now, such punishments—equalled only in
the dungeons of the Inquisition—may be *necessary* to preserve discipline in an army, a
great part of the materials of which, is res-
cued from the gallows, and transport ships;
for it is very common in England, when his
Majesty wants men, to offer a pardon to fel-
ons on condition of their entering the ser-

vice. It is a very general remark, that *the greatest cut throat makes the best soldier;* and I never heard that a man's being a scapegallows degraded him below the level of his comrades. And, indeed, why should it? He has only to follow his old trade with a new license. I repeat what I asserted, in one of my first numbers, that the man who engages in war, for no other motive than his pay, is but a hired cut throat—whether his epaulets be of gold or worsted,—and if the love of fame be his motive, his character is but little if any better.

The advocates of war plead, that it kills off many vile characters, and therefore it is necessary, in order to purge the state of its peccant humors. It must be allowed, that many such characters are disposed of by war ; but where one is got rid of, ten take his place—so that the state resembles the man, out of whom was cast an unclean spirit, —which returned with seven others, *worse than himself;* so that " the last state of that man was worse than the first." War produces the characters necessary for war. The evil increases as the war continues, and it would be as wise to expect to cleanse the blood by the itch, or any other loathsome disorder, as to expect to purify the body politic by war. The camp is infectious. The few, who go there virtuous, if they return at all, generally return vicious, and carry the infection into our peaceful hamlets and the bosom of families. The majority of an army is vicious, or it is not. If it is, how cruel to force or inveigle honest men, with steady habits, into scenes of corruption and depravity! If it is not, how inhuman to expose the virtuous and worthy, to pestilence and murder?—and what becomes of the argument of the friends of war, founded on the destruction of the vicious? Let them take which horn of the dilemma they choose, and they are still opposed to common sense.

NO. 23.

The consideration of the custom of War in a religious point of view.

I HAVE not yet considered War in a religious point of view, because I supposed that that was the peculiar province of the clergy, and because I concluded, that I was unable to do justice to the subject.

That the spirit of war is in direct opposition to the spirit of the gospel, no one, I believe, in these enlightened days, has the hardihood to deny. That the ambition of a military man is perfectly and entirely inconsistent with the humility of a christian, must be allowed by all. The age of ignorance and barbarism and chivalry—in which men sought to recommend themselves at once to the favor of Heaven and the smiles of the fair, by acts of murder, committed, not only on the heathen, whom it was thought a duty to destroy, but on each other—has passed away, though some of its delusions have not

entirely ceased. In the *dark ages*, courage
was the only quality thought worthy of admiration ; and the use of the sword and the
lance the only learning becoming a gentleman, and credoes, pater-nosters, and ave Ma-
rias, the only devotion of a christian, and the
fair sex fit for nothing but to adorn a tournament and crown the victors.

However poets and romancers may work
up the adventures of brave knights and fair
damsels into splendid pictures, to charm the
imagination of inexperienced youth, no man
would *now* hazard the ridicule of the age, by
wishing such scenes returned,—no philanthropist but must rejoice that mankind are,
in a *measure*, emancipated from a state of ignorance, vassalage and thraldom, little superior to the negro slavery of the present day ;
and no christian but must render devout
thanks that the " glorious gospel of the blessed God" has scattered the thick darkness,
which covered the nations. Yes, the change
which has been already effected, has been
wrought by the gospel of Peace ; and the
change which is yet to be made, will be effected by the same means. Every bible society
is in fact a peace society.

Yet much remains to be done. Much of
that blind admiration of personal courage,
without regard to end or object, remains.
Murder, havoc and desolation, yet, in some
degree, receive the countenance of christians,
and the approbation of the fair sex. Professing christians yet rush into the deadly con-

flict, and *glory* in sending fellow-immortals to that grave, where there is neither pardon nor repentance,—to that judgment seat for which they are totally unprepared,—to that place "where the worm dieth not, and the fire is not quenched"—whence "the smoke of their torment shall rise up forever and ever."

As I feel myself altogether unequal to this subject, I shall close this number, by a quotation from "the Herald of Peace," published in England. Vol. II. p. 173.

"Were warriors to die like the horses which bear them into the rage of battle, were there no existence after the present life, no account to be given in at a future tribunal, no heaven to be lost or gained, no region of unspeakable and eternal misery to be avoided or partaken of, then would the soldier's folly in throwing away his life be less conspicuous, and the prince's criminality in urging his subjects on to their destruction, be less heinous. But the case is not so. After death comes the judgment : after time is concluded comes eternity ; after the day of probation is ended, comes heaven or hell, as the unalterable, the eternal residence of every man. To die is at all times and under all circumstances, a solemn matter. To depart hence unpardoned, unsanctified, and consequently unsaved, is the prelude to weeping and wailing and gnashing of teeth for ever. Now, when we consider an army of one hundred thousand men marching on to a campaign, in which they will slay perhaps two-thirds of as numerous

10*

an army of their adversaries, and leave two-
thirds of their own number dead on the plain
—when we consider the awful profaneness
which pervades such a connected host of men
in their general manners, the rage and lust
and murder that operate in the hour of battle
and in the day of plunder—when we call to
mind, that in the very heat and full exercise
of all these unhallowed passions and pursuits
of their souls they are dismissed to the righteous tribunal of heaven, there to be judged
by Him who hath commanded all men to love
each other as brethren—when we read as from
the lips of this Judge himself, that there is
neither repentance nor reformation in the
grave, that at death he who is unholy must
remain unholy still, and he that is filthy must
remain filthy still, that nothing which defileth
can enter into his kingdom—when I say we
thus reflect as we gaze on the heaps of
slaughtered warriors, O what can charity itself furnish to sooth our grief or allay our
fears as to the final state of by far the greater portion of all who are thus untimely cut
off? What shadow of a plea worthy one moment's hearing can those princes and sena-
tors advance in justification of their conduct,
or in extenuation of all the accumulated and
eternal misery they have brought on so many
of their fellow creatures, whose immortality
is now their greatest curse, because they have
passed away from this state of probation un-
called by their Maker, and unprepared to
give up their account? They have closed

their period of time, but not repented—finished their days, but not reformed. They have died in the perpetration of acts which God has forbidden, and sealed, for ever sealed, their unspeakable, their eternal misery !"

NO. 24.

The same subject continued.

I RESUME the subject of my last number,—viz. the consideration of the custom of war, in a religious point of view—partly to allow myself an opportunity to apologize to the fair sex, for an error I had fallen into, rather from ignorance, than inclination.

In copying an abridgment of my 14th number, which the editor of the Friend of Peace did me the honor to insert in his valuable miscellany—in allusion to what I had remarked on female writers—he observes, " The author of this remark did not then " recollect," if he had seen, what has been written on this interesting subject by Mrs. Hamilton, Mrs. Barbauld, Mrs. Cappe, and Mrs. Schimmelpenninck. These are writers of no ordinary " eminence." They may not have written long essays on war; but each of them has written some things on this barbarous practice, which would do honor to any writer, whether male or female."

I must confess, that owing to my limited reading, I had not then ever seen any of the productions of the above-mentioned ladies on the subject of war; though I acknowledge their eminence. I render my most hearty thanks to Philo Pacificus, for his timely and welcome correction. In order to make the "amende honorable" to the sex, and because I feel conscious I cannot do better, I close this number by a quotation from a female writer of distinction, viz. the above-named Mrs. Schimmelpenninck. It is quoted from her "Biblical Fragments," into the Herald of Peace, Vol. II. p. 229.

"If the remarks above made are just, respecting the retribution of legislative justice, what room shall be found for the horrible devastations of war? By which, from the time of Cain, the first murderer, mankind, in the spirit of Cain, have presented the horrible spectacle of brethren of the same family, armed against each other! How dreadful is it to consider, that such scenes of human slaughter and butchery should still continue to desolate the earth; though the religion of the Prince of Peace has been preached for 1800 years! And that, although the armies mutually engaged in slaughtering each other, both, perhaps, profess that religion which bids them love as brethren, and which has declared, that "no murderer hath eternal life abiding in him;" and that, "he that saith he is in the light, and hateth his brother, is in darkness even until now;" a religion which has prohibited the practice not only of individual murder, but that of war, and which has forbidden it in every form, probably, in which it can be prohibited.

1st. In principle. " From whence come wars and fightings amongst you ?" (i. e. those professing to be Christians.) " Come they not hence, even of your lusts, that war in your members : ye lust, and have not ; ye kill, and desire to have, and cannot obtain ; ye fight and war, yet ye have not, because ye ask not."

2dly. In the outward act. " Thou shalt not kill." " No murderer hath eternal life abiding in him." " All they that take the sword shall perish by the sword." " Do violence to no man."

3dly. As to the spirit of war, when proceeding from vengeance. " Vengeance is mine ; I will repay, saith the Lord." " He that loveth not his brother, abideth in death." " Whosoever hateth his brother is a murderer." " He that hateth his brother is in darkness." " Love your enemies ; bless them that curse you ; do good to those that hate you, and pray for those that despitefully use you."

4thly. War is equally forbidden as a resort of self-defence. " Thou shalt not do evil, that good may come." " Cursed is he that trusteth in an arm of flesh." " Thou shalt not kill." " Till heaven and earth pass, one jot or one tittle shall in no wise pass from the law till all be fulfilled." " Wisdom is better than weapons of war."

5thly. As to authorizing others to break the divine law. " Whosoever, therefore, shall break one of these commandments and

shall teach men so, he shall be called the
least in the kingdom of heaven."

Accordingly, we find that, even under the
old covenant, which was less spiritual, and
in which many things were allowed for the
hardness of men's hearts; David, though a
man, in many respects, after God's own
heart, was not suffered to build the house of
God, BECAUSE HE WAS A MAN OF BLOOD. Well
might we be astonished, seeing that the horrors of war are thus in every possible form
forbidden, both as to the principle and the
outward act, that wars should still continue
to desolate Christendom! And still more
astonished might we well be, that in the
ranks of battle are to be found many men
who are undeniably Christians; and some
who are eminently, and, in other respects,
exemplarily so; and whose wish no doubt, it
is in all cases, to walk in obedience to Christ.
Whilst then, we cannot too strongly lay before our readers the enormity of the practice,
and its entire and total inconsistency with
Christian principles, we cannot too much also
bear in mind, nor inculcate the great allowance that is to be made for early education,
association, and habits; and the difficulty
and length of time before we submit habits,
in which we have been trained, as matters of
course, to the standard of general principles;
and, above all, to the standard of the sanc-
tuary. Christianity in our own hearts, as in
that of others; in governments, as in individuals, "is a light in a dark place;" but, bless-

ed be God! "it is a light that shineth more
and more unto the perfect day." Whilst,
then, we are bound faithfully to point out the
inconsistency of these things, we are not to
depart from the respect due to those otherwise excellent individuals, to whose consciences these truths have probably not been presented. We have but to look into our own
hearts, to see how possible it is to be truly a
believer, and yet to be a very imperfect believer, both as to instruction and practice.
Faith may be genuine, though the instruction
and practice are progressive. We wish, then,
clearly to be understood as meaning no inju-
rious or disrespectful reflections on those who
have not yet brought war to the test of scripture light. In how many points is our own
conscience now enlightened, on which it was
uninformed even a short time since; and in
how many more will it be enlightened, in
which it is now in entire obscurity! Far be
it from us not to grant the forbearance we so
much need. The word is as *the leaven;* it
may be truly hidden in the heart, though it
has not yet pervaded the whole of its avenues.
Many were, no doubt, in the days of Queen
Mary and Elizabeth, conscientious persecu-
tors, respectively of Protestants and Catho-
lics; who would now shudder at the thought.
We need go no further back than the excellent Mr. Newton, to find a truly good man
who for many years was unconvinced of the
iniquity of that trade of blood, the Slave
Trade. Sixty years ago, many no doubt ex-

cellent men, had never thought on its enormity : now, there are few, indeed, to be found,
even amongst men of common humanity, who
would advocate it.   Just so, we now believe,
that many of the most excellent men patron-
ize war.   But, blessed be God! the light of
the Prince of Peace is spreading; and the
number of those who are children of peace
is daily increasing.   In a century, may not
the children of God look back with surprise
on their past inconsistency ?"

NO. 25.

The same subject continued.

I MUST beg the indulgence of my readers
for leave to continue the subject of my two
last papers to a third communication, because
I feel desirous that abler pens than mine
should engage in shewing the inconsistency
of a spirit of war, with the doctrines and precepts of the Gospel. For this reason I would
make one more extract from the writings of
Mrs. Schimmelpenninck, from which it will
appear that she had already anticipated many
of my ideas on the subject of war.   I trust, it
may lead the attention of my fair countrywomen to the same subject, in hopes to excite
them to an emulation of her praise-worthy example:—for they have an influence, of which
they seem unconscious, and it is in their power, not only like the Sabine women to prevent
the slaughter of their husbands and fathers,
but by the careful education of their children,

and the encouragement they might give to peace principles, to banish war from civilized society.

"Nor have we reason to believe our hope vain, that the light is spreading : and in no country more rapidly than in our own. May we hail the light, and may we each, in our individual instance, seek to spread . it more abundantly ; and that not only by inculcating it preceptively, and by submitting the opposite principles to the touchstone of Scripture ; but above all, may we spread it by example ; by cultivating, in our own individual capacity, a meek and quiet spirit ; by not returning evil for evil, but good for evil. May we, as far as in us lies, endeavor to live peaceably with all men ; knowing " that the wrath of man worketh not the righteousness of God." If it must be that an alienation subsists, either in public parties or domestic circles, let not the spirit or the practice of alienation subsist with us ; and let no endeavor for peace be wanting on our side. If an offence be, let it not come through us ; let nothing be thought too dear a sacrifice for peace, but a good conscience. Never let us forget that we are disciples of that Almighty God, who took upon him human nature, to shed his blood for those who sinned against him ; and who, being sinned against, waited not to be entreated, but was the first to beseech them to be reconciled to God. Nor let the Christian only seek peace and ensue it himself, but seek to cultivate the spirit of

11

peace in his household. How many of the
amusements and employments furnished to
children, seem as though intended to stir up
every evil principle of violence and pride, ever latent in the human heart! The gun, the
drum, the sword, which is so often and so
injudiciously the child's first plaything; and
the classic pages, both of poets and historians, furnished by their masters, seem ex-
pressly calculated to foster every principle
of pride, resistance and rebellion; which is
most contrary to the spirit of Him who was
eminently meek and lowly in heart, and who
returned not evil for evil. How different
should be the course of that consistent parent who truly wishes his children to be followers of the Prince of Peace! Were every
Christian individual to bear these things in
his heart, how great a difference would the
face of society soon present! Though at
present the time seems afar off, let us not despair. The Christian has an encouragement
in his endeavors, which the man of the world
can never have in any mere temporal pur-
suit; the Word of God, the Spirit of God,
and the promise of God, go forth with him;
"nor shall God's Word return unto him
void, without having accomplished that for
which He sent it." The Christian, "who
sows in tears," may not see it in the body;
but "he shall one day," though in the spirit,
"see the abundant harvest." Nor is there
any cause in which the Christian may trust
with more confidence than in the holy cause

of peace; of Him who came, in a spiritual sense, to give peace on earth and good will to men; and whose religion, received into the heart, would also externally bear that fruit in the conduct; and that it will one day do so, we have the full promise, (Isaiah xi. 9.) "They shall not hurt nor destroy in all my holy mountain; for the earth shall be full of the knowledge of the Lord, as the waters cover the sea." (Chap. ii. 2—4.) "And it shall come to pass in the last days, that the mountain of the Lord's house shall be established in the top of the mountains, it shall be exalted above the hills; and all nations shall flow unto it. And many people shall go and say, Come ye, and let us go up to the mountain of the Lord, to the house of the God of Jacob, and he will teach us of his ways, and we will walk in his paths; for out of Zion shall go forth the law, and the word of the Lord from Jerusalem. And he shall judge among the nations, and shall rebuke many people; and they shall beat their swords into ploughshares, and their spears into pruning hooks: nation shall not lift up sword against nation, neither shall they learn war any more." Well may we then, in the mean time, address our Christian brethren and sisters in the concluding words of the prophet: (Isaiah ii. 5.) 'O house of Jacob, come YE, and let US walk in the light of the Lord.' "

NO. 26.

Inconsistent conduct of Christians.

No ONE, who fully believes the Holy Scriptures, can have the least doubt, that the time must assuredly come, when peace shall prevail over the whole earth—when "nation shall not lift up sword against nation, neither shall they learn war any more." Those who say, that this prophecy will not be fulfilled, deny the inspiration of the Scriptures. With such we have nothing to do, being persuaded, that they will "wax worse and worse." But I acknowledge, we are not to expect universal peace until the whole world shall be converted to the christian religion; and I fully believe that this universal conversion can never take place, until professing christians cease to outrage every principle of that gospel, which they are earnestly endeavoring to disseminate. What a glaring contrast between the principles of the christian religion and the practice of Christians, must strike the minds of the heathen, to whom the gospel is preached! How must such inconsistency put an insuperable bar to their conversion! How must every Heathen, like the emperor of China, be prejudiced against a religion, the professors of which, to use the words of the emperor, "have whitened all the countries, where they have obtained a footing, with human bones!"

It is not, principally, from the open oppos-

ers of christianity, nor from those, who
while they take the name, deny the power of
it, that we have most to fear : for happily,
the number of both is daily diminishing. But
our efforts are paralyzed by the inconsistent,
the unbelieving, and the lukewarm christian;
those, who say, " The time is not come that
the Lord's house should be built."—Those
who say, it is God's work, and nothing that
man can do will advance the predicted period.   It is useless to reason with such people,
until we see them *sincere* in their objections,
and that they use the same arguments, and
pursue the same conduct, in their own af-
fairs ; until we see them neglecting to sow in
the spring, because " the time is not come"
when they shall gather the crop, and believing nothing they can do will alter the decree
of God with respect to their harvest, and that
this decree will be · fulfilled, whether they
sow or not.   To such men I say, that *now* is
the time for exertion.   Say not ye, " There
are yet four months, and then cometh the
harvest ?   Behold, I say unto you, lift up
your eyes, and look on the fields ; for they
·are white already to harvest.   And he that
reapeth receiveth wages, and gathereth fruit
unto life eternal; that both he that soweth,
and he that reapeth, may rejoice together."
Yes, " the time, yea even the set time, to favor Zion is come."   Never, since the advent
of the Prince of Peace, has there been a season more auspicious for promoting the principles of peace, and the friends of peace
11*

ought to snatch the golden opportunity.
Peace prevails almost throughout the world.
The passions seem lulled to rest. The time
is past, when military glory was the only
path to honor and preferment. Christians
of every sect are dropping their contentions;
and are emulous only, who shall do most to
advance the Redeemer's kingdom in the
world. The savage is tamed, and the war
club is suspended in the missionary hall: and
we have reason to exclaim, what hath God
wrought! Light among nominal christians
is extending. Bible societies are sending the
precious word of God to every man's door;
the tract is to be seen in every cottage; and
sabbath schools are teaching children the
principles of the peaceable religion of Jesus.
*The next generation will be different from the
last.* All this in the short term of less than
twenty years! and not a step taken without
man's instrumentality! Is this a time of despair—a time for lukewarmness—a time for
a christian to fold his arms, and look on to
see others made God's honored instruments? Morality forbids it. Philanthropy
forbids it. Religion forbids it. God forbids
it. .No, let us press forward. "Success is
as sure as the gospel is true."

NO. 27.

Objections to peace principles considered.

It is objected against the friends of peace,
that they will never accomplish their object,

and that there will be more or less war, so
long as the world shall stand. I have endeavored, in my last, to refute that objection, by
arguments drawn from the word of God, the
sure word of prophecy. But to those on
whom such arguments will not prevail, we
may adduce moral reasoning and historical
facts.

The great objection against the promulgation of the principles of peace is, that they
would render the nation that receives them
a prey to more warlike neighbors. This argument is not supported by fact, nor by reasoning from the common principles of moral
suasion. On the contrary, those nations that
have made the greatest military preparations
have, in consequence of those very preparations, been most frequently engaged in war;
while those nations, which have shown no
will, nor even ability, to act on the offensive,
have been most at peace. Monarchs make
war chiefly for glory, and there is no glory
in attacking the peaceable and unoffending.
If they make war for an extension of territory; they instantly excite the jealousy of other warlike states, who will never see a peaceable neighbor conquered, and by that means,
the power of another state, already too strong,
increased. Facts, drawn from the history
of Europe, might be quoted to prove these
assertions; but that would too much enlarge
my communication, and it would be unnecessary to the greater part of my readers. I
would just observe, how few have been the

changes in the territory of the European
states, for the last hundred years, after all
their wars. It is true Poland has been dis-
membered ;—but Poland was a nation of warriors, and retained more of the. ancient feu-
dal and warlike manners than any other
state in Europe ; which proves, that a warlike spirit is at least *no better* defence of a nation than a peaceable disposition. On the
contrary, the ancient Hanse towns flourished
beyond all example, until they became a mili-
itary power, which soon ruined them ; and
the modern Hanse towns, though weak and
without a military force, have stood unmoved
amid all the convulsions of Europe. It is
true, that in 1806 Hamburg was taken by
the French ; yet it suffered less than more
warlike cities.

But we have another forcible consideration
to offer, which is, that it is not probable, that
peace principles will prevail in one country
alone, to the exclusion of all others. On the
contrary, we see that the light of truth on
this subject, which arose simultaneously in
this country and in England, has spread already, though in dim twilight, not only over
a great part of Europe, but has dawned in
the East Indies : has enlightened the Islands
of the Pacific ocean, and glimmered even in
South America. Whatever may have been
the first intentions of the Holy Alliance, their
unholy conduct, in making war in Spain, has
roused a burst of indignation and contempt
in the civilized world, which is a sure indica-

tion of a great change in public opinion, and
which the crowned heads themselves cannot
but feel. Peace principles are spreading wider and wider every day; and the nations
most forward in adopting them, will cover
themselves with a glory, which will endure,
long after the names of heroes and of conquerors shall have rotted in oblivion.

The influence of every individual, who engages in the cause of peace, however weak
his talents, extends from pole to pole; though
that influence may not be perceptible. Vast
as is the ocean, take one drop from it, and it
is no longer the same. What then must be
the influence of such nations as Great Britain
and America—the most enlightened, the most
free, and the most happy in the world? It
is great, powerful and overwhelming; and
it must and will prevail. We see what their
influence has been on the slave trade—no
christian nation now dares openly defend
it. Their influence has been felt in the
dissemination of Christian knowledge, by
bible, missionary and tract societies: and
shall it not be felt, when they endeavor to
diffuse the very spirit of all these institutions?

As we have encouragement, from the fact
that the slave trade, religious persecutions,
witchcraft, and other delusions have been
abolished; so we have encouragement from
the fact, that where nations have adopted the
peace policy, it has succeeded. I have already mentioned the Hanse towns, and for-

merly alluded to the Quaker government of
Pennsylvania, which preserved peace and
quietness for 70 years among hordes of savages; and also to the history of the Jews,
who left their cities defenceless when they
went up to Jerusalem, yet no one desired
their land. What then have christians and
philanthropists to do, but to press forward,
and secure a glorious and bloodless victory ?

NO. 28.

An appeal to all orders and conditions of Men.

THERE is a loud call on all orders and
conditions of men, to seize with avidity the
present favorable season for disseminating
the principles of peace. Let us not wait until the angry passions of mankind are excited
by designing men; until the alarm of war
shall be sounded, and the remonstrances of
reason and religion drowned in " the confus-
ed noise of the warrior." Then,

> " You might as well go stand upon the beach,
> And bid the sea to 'bate its wonted roar;
> You might as well plead pity with the wolf."

In the present quiet state of the world, no
age, sex or condition is exempted from the
imperious duty of endeavoring to make " our
peace like a river," gently flowing and wid-
ening, until it becomes " a sea without a
shore."

Are you a legislator? Use every means

in your power to encourage a pacific disposition toward other nations. The late arrange-
ment between this country and Great Britain,
by which privateering against each other is
abolished, is a glorious victory of the principles of peace. The mutual right of searching
vessels suspected of being engaged in the
slave trade, is another victory : for slavery
and war are almost synonymous.* Abolish
slavery, and many wars in Africa will cease.
Abolish war, and much slavery in Europe
will cease.

Are you a private citizen? Make the
most of your suffrage in favor of peace. Never cast a vote in favor of a man who has been
guilty of private war, or an encourager of
public hostilities. Seek those *men*, as well as
things, that make for peace,—considering
that "righteousness exalteth a nation ; but
sin is a reproach to any people." Can you
conscientiously vote for one, who has broken
the laws of his country by private revenge,
and imbrued his hands in the blood of a fellow citizen, and who *glories* in it? Or can
you support a man for office, who is for settling every trivial difference with a foreign
nation, by the sword, regardless of the misery
he brings on his own country, and the danger
to which he exposes your property, liberty,
morals and eternal salvation? Bear in mind

---

* These arrangements, which were in progress when
this essay was written, we have reason to lament, have not
yet taken effect ; Great Britain having neglected to con-
firm one and the senate of the United States the other.

that the reformation of a nation from warlike
to peaceable habits, like all other reforma-
tions, must begin with *the people.* Rulers,
under every form of government, are inclined
to war, because it strengthens their hands,
increases their power, flatters their ambition,
enlarges their patronage, and fills their pockets.

Are you an author ?—a poet ?—a man of
letters ?   Your influence on public opinion is
great.   It was said by an Athenian, that he
cared not who made the laws, so that he
made the music, intimating that music had
more influence on popular opinion than the
laws had.   If this is the case with bare sound,
how much more when sound is accompanied
with sentiment !   The effect of " national
airs," as they were called, in arousing a blood-
thirsty spirit, was witnessed in the French
revolution.   The verses of Homer and Virgil,
and the prose of Xenophon and Livy, have
done much to keep up a war spirit in the
world ; and it is not to be doubted, that an
opposite character of their works would have
had a contrary effect.   A pastoral song rep-
resenting the happy life of a Swiss peasant,
and imitating the looing of cows, when sung
among the Swiss soldiers, in the French army, had such an effect as to make them desert in great numbers, so that the French
officers prohibited the singing of it on pain
of death.   If then you are an author, and a
friend of peace, you ought not to omit any
opportunity of giving your testimony in its

favor; and whenever you are called on to describe the circumstances of a battle, or the character of a warrior by profession, it is your duty to put both in a proper point of view; that the tender minds of youth, which are just taking their bent, may not receive from you a wrong direction. Charles 12th, of Sweden, while studying Latin in his youth, had his mind influenced by reading the life of Alexander the great by Quintus Curtius; so that the Roman historian became accessary to all the murders which Charles committed in Europe.

Are you a soldier by profession? Remember the injunction of John the Baptist, the forerunner of our Saviour : "Do violence to no man." Examine the principles of the Christian religion with impartiality, and then if you can conscientiously follow your trade,—do it. If not,—seriously ask yourself this question : "What shall it profit a man to gain the whole world and lose his own soul ?"

The shortness of my remaining paper admonishes me, that it is time to draw towards a conclusion. In fine then, there is no station in society, in which a man may not be useful in disseminating the principles of peace. And if he does no more than barely give his testimony in favor of peace principles by joining a peace society, and purchasing and distributing peace tracts, it will not lose its effect, nor will he lose his reward.

In conversing a few days ago, with a gentleman of talents and influence, and also a professor of religion, I asked him if he belonged to the peace society ? No.—I expressed my surprise. " I have not the least doubt," said he, " that the custom of war is in direct opposition to the Christian religion; and I am so fully convinced, that I have no occasion for reading any thing further on the subject." He might as well have said, that as he was perfectly well convinced of the truth of the christian religion, he had no occasion for a bible. It is as much the duty of every friend of peace to give public testimony in favor of it, as it is of a christian to make a profession of religion. By becoming a member of a peace society, a man puts the weight of his character into the scale of peace. By buying their publications, he increases their funds. By reading them, he strengthens his principles,—fills his mouth with arguments, —learns the most effectual way of furthering the cause of peace, and how to act in concert with others. By circulating them, he serves the cause of peace by making known its principles, and very probably will make converts. I speak from experience ; for it was by reading a few numbers of the Friend of Peace, casually lent me by a friend, that my attention was called to the subject, and I renounced my former sentiments, and became an advocate for peace.

NO. 29.

Appeal to professors of Religion.

I WOULD address a few words on the subject of permanent and universal peace to professors of religion.

Too long have you left the cause of peace to bare philanthropists and men of the world. It is full time to ask you, " What do ye more than others ?" You may answer, that you do all you can to spread the Gospel ; that you are a member of a missionary, a bible and a tract society, and probably of an education and Sunday school society, and that you subscribe for the religious publications of the day. You have done well, and, I have no doubt, reap a full recompense of reward in your bosoms. But how can Christian nations expect the blessing of God on their exertions, to extend the Gospel of peace, while they " bite and devour one another ;" while they prize more the honor which cometh from men, than that which cometh from God. While christians worship military glory, with what face can they pretend to convert the Hindoo from the worship of Juggernaut, not more foolish, and less bloody, than their own. The reproach of the Emperor of China yet tingles in my ears. Yes, " Christians have whitened, with human bones, the countries they have conquered, or converted." If men were to be *dragooned* into the kingdom of Heaven, then indeed, the Knights of the Teutonic order, and the "booted apostles" of later times, might do much execution. But our religion is "*pure, peaceable, gentle, easy to be entreated, full of mercy and of good fruits.*" What will the inquiring Hindoo think, when he sees our conduct to each other? It is more natural for him, to judge of the Christian religion, by the conduct of its professors, than by its precepts. How must he detest the religion of those, who have sailed thousands of leagues, to rob and plunder him, and then fight with each other for his spoils?

Now, what have you done to aid the cause of peace? On the contrary, are there not many of you, who are not ashamed to appear vain of military habiliments, and to glory in military titles? I do not say, that you cannot do this, and be christians. But I do say that your *practice* is in direct opposition to the religion you profess. I put it to your consciences whether you can return from a military review,—from such scenes of profanity and intemperance as are there generally exhibited,—from the loaded table, the flowing bowls, the equivocal toasts, the indecent jests and songs, and ribaldry, which too frequently succeed—can you return from such scenes, and call your family around you, and close the day by prayer, in a spirit and temper agreeable to the religion you profess? From what I have seen of militia reviews and balls, I am of opinion, that the latter are purity itself, when compared to the others. How can you

reconcile the humility, meekness and benevolence of the christian character—which teach-
es us "in honor to prefer one another"—with
the pride, contention, intrigue and cabal of a
militia election, in which every one endeavors
"utterly to supplant his brother?" Though
a proud and vain-glorious worldling may gratify his ambition, by displaying his epaulets in
the tented field, it is difficult to conceive
what congruity with his pious feelings, a
humble christian can find, if placed in the
same situation.

When we look into your houses, how frequently do we see their walls hung with pictures of sieges and battles, and portraits of
generals and conquerors, and the books in
your children's hands, of that description
which cherishes military ardor, and gives
them a thirst for military glory, and their
very toys of a warlike character.

"These things ought not so to be." There
ought to be some difference between the professors of the peaceable religion of Jesus
Christ, and those who worship the god of this
world. By such conduct you sanction war
with all its horrid consequences : you lower
the standard of christian perfection, and
bring a reproach on the holy name by which
you are called.

To pass from the things which you have
done to those which you have left undone, I
would again inquire what you have done to
advance the principles of peace ? You believe that the custom of war is in direct op-

position to the christian religion. What have
you done to check its progress—what to countenance and support those philanthropists
and christians, who are endeavoring to stem
the current, and give a right direction to public opinion? Shall this work be taken out
of your hands by men of the world? Shall
they go before you in inculcating the principles of the religion you *profess*? Will you
be content with the profession, and leave the
practice to them? But little is required of
you. Had you been bidden to "do some
great thing," you probably would have done
it with alacrity. But it is necessary only to
give your testimony—to pray heartily for the
cause—to contribute a few cents annually to
the funds of the Peace Society—to read the
tracts they publish yourself, and lend them to
your neighbors. Could you not induce two,
three, or more of your town, or neighborhood to join in a reading peace society; and
by an annual subscription of twelve, twenty-
five, or fifty cents, procure the tracts which
have been published in this country, or perhaps from England? You have this to encourage you, that you cannot fail of success.

Perhaps the labor of drafting a constitution, or a diffidence of putting yourself forward, may keep you back. In order to ob-
viate this difficulty, the proprietor of the Mirror has generously engaged to print a sufficient number of copies of a draft of a constitution, which has lately been adopted by a
peace society in the interior of this state, and

to distribute them gratis with his paper.
Any alteration you please may be made.
Make the attempt, and the success will sur-
pass your expectation.*

There is an advantage attending peace societies which should not be overlooked:
which is, that all persons, of every sect and
denomination of religion can unite in them—
professors and non-professors,——christians
and philanthropists; and it will be found,
that the greater are your exertions in favor
of peace, the greater will be the peace among
yourselves. "The middle wall of partition,"
which has too long separated christians, will,
in this instance, be "so lowered, that they
may shake hands over it;" and if there be
any strife, it will be who shall do most to favor "the things which make for peace, and
things whereby you may edify one another."

On this ground also, those who allow the
lawfulness of *defensive* war, can heartily
meet those who deny it. All christians must
agree in denouncing *offensive* war as perfectly inconsistent with the precepts of their religion. Let them earnestly endeavor to disseminate the principles of peace, and then
there will be no occasion to differ about the
lawfulness of defensive wars, for they will

---

* The proprietor of the Christian Mirror caused a good
number of these drafts to be distributed. One peace society has been since formed, which has adopted this constitution; and some others are in progress. A copy, with a
little alteration, will be found in the appendix.

Since the first edition has been printed about ten new
societies have been founded on similar principles.

cease. I call on you, professing christians,
to exert yourselves to " do what you can"
to advance the cause of Peace; and may
" the God of all peace" crown your labors
with success.

NO.' 30.

Appeal to Ministers of the Gospel.

IT is with much diffidence and respect,
that I attempt to address the Rev. Clergy,
of all denominations, on the subject of war.
But as I think that my series of essays would
be incomplete without an appeal to them,—
and that they have not " done what they
could" in the cause of Peace,—and that duty
is paramount to all other considerations, I
shall venture to suggest to them a few considerations.

It is true, indeed, that the gospel proclaims " Peace on earth and good will to
men ;" and that the principles of peace are
strongly inculcated from the beginning to the
end of it. It follows, of course, that whenever they preach the gospel, they must, if
faithful, inculcate the principles of peace.
But the fault is, that they fail in the application of those principles to actual conduct.
Nay, holy prelates have even laid aside the
mitre, and buckled on the helmet, and drawn
the sword, and rushed into the thickest of
the fight. Others, of each contending party,
have contented themselves with thundering
anathemas against the heads of their enemies,

and praying God to grant them the victory;
—so that, in war, we have cannon against
cannon, squadron against squadron, anathema
against anathema, and prayer against prayer.
I believe that in our army, during the late
war, there were no chaplains. Perhaps the
utter inconsistency of war with the Christian
religion, is becoming more and more appa-
rent. They are, however, continued in the
navy, and I have been acquainted with some
of them ; but do not wish, at present, to say
any thing of their character or conduct.

It is not for what *our* clergy do, but for
what they leave undone, that I think their
attention should be called to this subject. I
have never heard but two sermons on the
custom of war; one for, and the other against
it. Now is not this a culpable omission ? If
the spirit and practices of war be in direct
opposition to the spirit and precepts of the
gospel, should not the people be told so ? I
apprehend that "the fear of man, which
bringeth a snare," prevents many from " de-
claring the whole counsel of God." But it
should be remembered, that Felix trembled
at the preaching of Paul ; and that " God's
word will not return unto him void, but will
accomplish the purpose whereunto it is sent."
I would humbly suggest the propriety of
preaching, at least, one sermon in a year
against the antichristian practice of war ; and
that, at some stated season of the year. And
perhaps no time is so proper as Christmas,
which, by common consent of most sects of

Christians, is acknowledged as indicative of
the period when angels descended to proclaim
peace and good will.

There is another view of this subject, to
which, Rev. Fathers, I would venture to call
your attention. For other benevolent pur-
poses, the united prayer of God's people has
ascended to Heaven as incense; and, we have
reason to believe, has not ascended in vain.
'One day in every month is set apart for the
special purpose of prayer, that God would
bless his word among the Heathen. Would
it not be well, for Christians to unite in prayer,
at least one day in the year, that God would
be pleased to remove from the world the
scourge of war ? We pray that the idols of
the Heathen may be cast to the " bats and the
moles"—should we not pray that the idol of
military glory may share the same fate ? Has
it not been owing to the deficiency of our
prayers, that the friends of peace have not
met with much greater success ? Prayer has
not been made to God for them ; though he
has the hearts of rulers and of all other men
in his hands, and can turn them whither he
will, " even as the rivers of water are turned."
Should not our public prayer be offered, that
the hearts of *our* rulers in particular, may be
inclined to peace? You are as the mouth of
the people to God,—but alas, how seldom
have you led the public devotions to this object in particular ! Let me venture to recommend, that at your associations, and church
conferences, something may be done, and
some resolutions offered on this subject.

I would venture to propose, for your consideration, one other measure : which is, that each association of ministers should resolve itself into a peace society. By doing this, you would give your testimony in favor of peace. By a moderate annual contribution, you would aid the funds of the peace societies, and furnish yourselves with their tracts and pamphlets, which could be exchanged at every meeting of the association.

Could you not aid the cause of peace by establishing peace societies in your parishes ? You need not fear a failure in the attempt. Should you recommend the measure, it would surely be adopted—at least by the members of your churches. A very moderate contribution, say of 10, 12, or 30 cents per annum, would furnish you with all the peace tracts. Do you not think, that this would be a good thing ?—and if you know it to be good, and do it not, what is the inference ?

There is one other subject to which I would call your attention ; though I feel some hesitation, on account of the difference of opinion which prevails among you. But, like the Buzite in Job, " I will answer also on my part, I also will shew mine opinion. For I am full of matter ; the spirit within me constraineth me—Let me not, I pray you, accept any man's person." The subject is, the attendance of clergymen, as chaplains, at military reviews. I would, with deference, ask —what congruity with your sacred office do you find in the tented field ? Surrounded as you are by levity, profaneness, and intemperance, is not your address to the throne of grace a solemn mockery ? I have been informed that at a review in this state, before the time for forming the hollow square to attend worship had arrived, many of the men, —whether officers or privates I am not informed,—were so merry, that it was thought best to omit both the *evolution* and the *ceremony*. When you retire from the field to the table, do you not hear a voice sounding in your ears, " What doest thou here, Elijah ?" It is true, your presence may, at first, impose some restraint on those who fear you more than God ; but soon your voice is drowned in intemperate mirth, and the jingling of glasses and the proclaiming of toasts, and your person obscured by clouds of tobacco smoke. Now, if the parson takes the hint to be off, it is well ; if not, restraint soon ceases ; and the passions, bursting all bounds, rush forth with the greater impetuosity. Now I would ask again, what is there in these scenes, which is in congruity with your sacred function ? I do not say, that pious ministers may not perform the duties of a chaplain ; and perhaps the scenes exhibited at a review, are not *always* so bad as above described ; but I do think, and hope, that they have some twinges of conscience all the while, and that they would gladly be excused ; but that they fear to offend the officers, who are frequently influential men in their parishes ; but whether they ought to fear man rather than God, I

leave them to decide. I acknowledge it must
be a cross, to decline the office of chaplain,
when that compliment is paid them,—but
there are so few crosses laid on the shoulders
of the clergy of our days, that they ought
not to refuse to take up those which lie in
their way. If the subject were referred to
the consideration of an association; and they
should resolve on not accepting the office of
chaplain,—at least until intemperance were
banished from our military musters,—the re-
sponsibility would be more divided, and the
refusal made more easy; and yet the regiments may not be destitute of chaplains.
The above remarks express only my own private opinion, and perhaps I am wrong; but
I am open to conviction. Under my present
impressions, however, I cannot help thinking,
that as the matter is now conducted, a clergyman who accepts the office of chaplain to a
regiment, lessens his own personal respect,—
lowers the standing of the clergy, and dimin-
ishes the reverence due to their sacred func-
tions. And further than this, I think that it
is full as proper, for a clergyman to ask a
blessing on a card table, open a ball with a
prayer, or sing psalms at a theatre, as to appear in his canonicals at a military review.

NO. 31.

Appeal to the Female Sex.

BEFORE I close the series of essays, in
which I have been engaged, I cannot refrain
13

from making one more appeal to the female
sex, because I know the benevolence of their
general character, and the influence they have
over the other sex.

——" What mortal can deny
When suppliant beauty begs ?' '——

That you, my fair countrywomen, should
love courage and magnanimity, is natural
and right ;—but the indiscriminate praise
which your sex formerly bestowed, and many continue to bestow, on bare ferocious
courage, has done much to kindle and fan the
flames of war. We have reason to hope
that a more auspicious era is approaching.
In some parts of our country, there are female peace societies, that use their influence
to quench the thirst for military glory, and
lessen the evils of war. This is worthy of
imitation; and those who are foremost in the
good work are no less the friends of their
own sex, than of ours—for it is the interest
no less than the duty of your sex to discour-
age war. True,—thanks to the daily increasing influence of the peaceable principles
of the Christian religion,—your persons are
no longer—at least in Christendom,—considered as spoils of war, and do not become
the objects of a sordid and horrible traffic.
You are seldom exposed to those insults
worse than death, which, in ancient times,
even the most civilized nations permitted
their soldiers to inflict on you. And it is not
very often that your dwellings are destroyed,

and your property wasted, by an invading
army. Yet you are vulnerable in the persons of your friends of our sex; and by the
long continuance of war, you are lowered in
the estimation, in which we ought ever to
hold you; for, however military glory may
commence by courting your smiles, it ends,
—perhaps disgusted by satiety,—in neglecting and despising them. For, whatever
works of fiction, chivalry, and romance may
say to the contrary, the truth is, that war
blunts the feelings of those who are engaged
in it, and the heart becomes so callous, by
the frequent exhibition of female sufferings,
that they pass unregarded, or become objects
of sport and derision.

In support of this assertion, I adduce the
following extracts, from an account of Gen.
Matthews' *glorious* campaign against Tipoo
Sultan.

"Every man in Onore was put to the
sword. The carnage was great: we trampled thick on dead bodies that were strewed
in the way. It was rather shocking to humanity; but such are but secondary considerations to a soldier, whose bosom glows
with heroic glory, and are thought only accidents of course."

At the time Anampour was taken by
storm, says Lieut. Sheen, "when a practicable
breach was effected, orders were issued for a
storm and no quarters, which were immediately put into execution, and every man put
to the sword except one horseman, who made

his escape, after being wounded in three different places. A dreadful sight then presented itself; above four hundred beautiful women, either killed, or wounded with the bayonet, expiring in one another's arms, while the private soldiers were committing every kind of outrage, and plundering them of their jewels, the officers not being able to restrain them. The troops were, however, severely reprimanded for it. I had almost forgot, that some of the women, rather than be torn from their relations, threw themselves into large [water] tanks, and were drowned." Undoubtedly, this Lieut. Sheen is a great favorite among those ladies, who admire " *heroic glory ;*" which gives no quarters, even to " beautiful women ;" who, while expiring in each other's arms, " killed or wounded," not by chance shot, but, " with the bayonet," were subjected to " *every kind of outrage*" from a brutal soldiery ; " the officers not being able to restrain them," or, more probably, setting them the example, and therefore " the troops were severely *reprimanded*," as their only punishment.   It is remarkable with what sang froid our brave lieutenant, whose bosom glowed with *heroic glory*, almost forgot to mention, that some of these beautiful women, rather than to be torn from their relatives, or, more likely, to disappoint the brutal lust of their savage enemy—threw themselves into large tanks, where they were drowned.   After this, we are not surprised to hear, that, rather than fall into the hands of *Christians*, the wives of the Sultan destroyed themselves. Oh, merciful Jesus, are these miscreants thy professed followers! With what countenance—with what hope of success, can missionaries preach the Gospel of Peace to those very people, who have suffered so much from those who bear thy name? That christian missionaries have so little success in India, is most probably owing to the countenance which christians give to war, and their love of "heroic glory." War, in one day, undoes more than missionaries can do in an age. And will my Christian country-women smile on war? If you have no pity on our sex, will you have none on your own, and on the souls of perishing heathen? However, as christians, you disapprove of the suicide committed by these pagan ladies, can you help admiring their modesty, which preferred death to violation? And can you suppress your horror and detestation of the custom of war, in which such atrocities are "thought only accidents of course?"

I was once a fellow boarder with a French envoy, famous for his barbarity and success in the civil wars of his own country. This wretch boasted, as I was told, that he had committed crimes which decency forbids me to name; and the writer heard him brag, even in the presence of ladies, of the many favors he had received from my fair countrywomen, and how much the country was indebted to him for an increase of its population. He also displayed to me and other boarders,

13*

a great profusion of female ornaments, of
diamonds and jewelry, which I have good
reason to conclude were the spoils of La
Vendee. I felt very indignant at the time.
But if you ladies, prefer such characters ; if
you choose to confer on them your smiles and
your favors, no one has a *right* to prevent
you. But I think it wonderful, that you have
not more consideration, for the interest and
dignity of your sex. When you honor and
glorify warriors barely for their exploits,—
when you rejoice at victories, which are
always attended by misery and anguish,—
by widows' tears, and virgins' shrieks, and
mothers' groans—you encourage robbery and
murder. That the baser part of your sex
should rejoice at the exploits of highwaymen
and pirates, and share their spoils, is not to
be wondered at; but that christian *ladies*—
ladies of delicacy and sentiment, should rejoice at and honor crimes which differ from
the others only by their magnitude, cannot
be accounted for by the light of nature.

I do not consider the above-mentioned
general worse than his master,—I mean Napoleon the great. What was his respect for
your sex, when he repudiated Josephine, and
married Maria Louisa ?—when he dissolved
the connexion between his brother Jerome,
and our silly country-woman, who, blinded
by the glare of military glory, wedded a mon-
key—instead of a man,—because he was brother to a conqueror ?—when he would have
forced another brother to divorce his wife,

and marry for state policy. Yet in this
christian land, where we profess to follow the
commands of him, who said, "Whosoever
shall put away his wife, and marry another,
committeth adultery;" in this republican
country, where we revolt at the very name of
legitimacy, I have heard this conduct excused;
and that too by ladies of high standing,—on
the pretence, that it was necessary for him, to
have *legitimate* offspring to succeed to his
throne, and to form great alliances to support
it,—though it was founded on opposition to
legitimacy—so inconsistent are the advocates
of war, and the admirers of military glory.

I need not, however, extend my remarks,
already too prolix. I have no doubt but that
a great majority of my fair countrywomen
are fully convinced, that the custom of war is
opposite to the christian religion, and hostile
to the interest, dignity and happiness of your
sex. But what have you done to aid the
cause of peace? You can do much, and
much it is your duty to do. If there is no
female peace society in your neighborhood,
you can commence one; if there is, you can
join it. The effect of your thus giving your
decided testimony in favor of peace, would
be very considerable. By distributing peace
tracts,—by laying them before your fathers,
husbands, and sons, you would serve the
cause. By persuading those, over whom you
have an influence, to become members of
peace societies—by the careful education of
your children—by removing from them all

those toys, amusements, pictures, music and
books which tend to inflame military ambition—by yourselves abstaining from martial
songs and airs—by all these means, you may
be fellow workers with God, and blessed and
honored instruments in his hands, for de-
stroying the strong holds of military glory,
and abolishing the custom of war. You have
a talent put into your hands, and remember,
that for your improvement of it, the God of
peace will call you to account.

NO. 32.

Conclusion.

I now come to the conclusion of the series
of essays which I undertook to write. I have
endeavored to show the origin and causes of
war,—among which, the *love of military glory* is the most prominent;—to point out
some of its evils and atrocities, and the absolute inconsistency of the custom of war with
the Christian religion. I have also proposed
remedies for the evil,—which are, principally, that every friend of Man should, for himself, read and consider on the subject; and,
both individually, and in concert with other
Christians and philanthropists, do what he
can, to disseminate correct sentiments;—
should give the weight of his character to the
cause of peace, and assist to tear the mask
from the hideous monster, *Military Ambition,*
and expose its naked deformity to its infatuated worshippers;—that the female sex should

not only assist in this benevolent work, but be foremost in this "labor of love," so congenial to the benevolence of their hearts; and that they should use the powerful influence they have over our sex, for the mutual happiness of both.

I know that many will consider me a visionary and an enthusiast. So the world thought Luther and Calvin, Wilberforce and Clarkson. Not that I have the vanity and presumption to compare myself with those venerable characters; or have any pretensions to originality in my endeavors to promote "permanent and universal peace;"—but I know, that God can bless the feeblest means; and *I know*, that we have *his promise*, that the time will come, when "nation shall not lift up sword against nation; neither shall they learn war any more:—*for the mouth of the Lord of Hosts hath spoken it.*" As great changes have been wrought in public opinion, as any which is contemplated by the friends of peace;—and this change must begin with the people. Luther might as well have expected reformation to commence with the court of Rome, as for us to suppose that rulers,—especially absolute rulers—will be favorable to peace. All despotic governments are founded on force; and this force is perpetuated by armies; and these armies are supported by war; but

"War is a game, that, were their subjects wise,
Kings would not play at."

When wars shall become unpopular, they

must cease in free countries, and they cannot long continue even in absolute monarchies,—but the world will never be free, until " wars and fightings" cease. It is, therefore, the imperious duty of the republican, the philanthropist, and the Christian, to do all they can to disseminate the principles of Peace. I have been actuated by these motives, to cast my " mite" into the scale of peace. If it has any effect, I shall be thankful. If it has not, I shall still have the satisfaction of having " done what I could."

But there has been an evident and general change in public opinion, respecting the custom of war; and the principles of peace are steadily and constantly progressing. What if the present generation does not see the full accomplishment of God's promise ;—is that a reason for despair ? " Though it tarry, wait for it : because it will surely come." What if we cannot accomplish all we wish, —is that a reason why we should do nothing ? If all the exertions of all the peace societies and philanthropists in the world should prevent one war, or even one battle,—in which thousands of immortal souls are precipitated into a miserable eternity, and as many thousands bereaved of near and dear relatives,— the reward would infinitely exceed the labor.

I now take my leave of the public. If I have hurt the feelings of any individual, I am sorry for it. It has not been my intention; —for having no personal antipathies to indulge, none of my remarks have been made

for personal application.   I am an enemy to
no one, except so far as he is an enemy to my
brethren of the human family.   I wish temporal and eternal happiness to all ; and if I
know my own heart, I have been influenced
to write these essays, by a love of "peace on
earth and good will to men."

APPENDIX.

—◆—

It often happens, that some few persons, residing in a neighborhood, village, or town, are desirous of forming themselves into a peace society, for the purpose of more readily obtaining the works, which have been published on the subject of *permanent and universal peace ;* but are deterred from forming such an association, by the diffidence which a person feels, of putting himself forward to form a constitution. For this reason the following is offered to their consideration, taken chiefly from the constitutions of societies actually existing, and subject to any alteration, which local circumstances may render necessary.

It is hoped that *ministers of the gospel of peace*, of all denominations, will endeavor to form societies, in their respective churches and congregations. A very few—even four or five, would be sufficient to begin with. These would form a nucleus, around which many others would probably gather, and in time, a numerous society grow out of a small beginning. It is surely worth the trial, the expense would be small, and probably, the effect would be great.

14

CONSTITUTION

OF THE

PEACE SOCIETY OF

WE the subscribers, being convinced of the evil tendency and unchristian nature of a warlike spirit, and being persuaded that wars ought to cease, and finally will cease, to the ends of the earth; and believing that this desirable event will be brought about by God's blessing on human means, and a change in popular opinion, respecting the lawfulness of war, and the nature of military glory; and desiring to become instrumental in abolishing the custom of war, and wishing further to instruct ourselves and our neighbors, by reading and circulating books and tracts on the subject of Peace and War, do form ourselves into a society, on the following conditions, viz.

Art. 1. This society shall be called the —— Peace society of ——.

2. Each subscriber to the amount of —— cents per annum, shall be a member of this society; and each subscriber of —— dollar— shall be a life member.

3. This society shall meet annually, on the —————— day of ————, at such hour and place as the board of managers may appoint.

4. The concerns of the society shall be conducted by a President, a Vice-President, a Secretary, (who shall be also librarian,) and a Treasurer, (who shall also be collector and agent for procuring tracts.) The above named officers shall constitute the board of Managers, any three of whom shall form a quorum.*

5. The funds of the society shall be exclusively employed in the purchase of books and tracts on Peace and War, calculated to advance the interests of Peace, for the use of the members, and for circulation.

6. The first meeting of this society shall be on the ———— day of ———— next, at which meeting the above-mentioned officers shall be chosen, and any alteration made in this constitution which a majority of the members present may think necessary.

7. At any annual meeting of the society any change in the constitution may be made, provided notice of the contemplated change be given in the warning for calling the meeting at least three weeks before the time of meeting; and provided that three-fifths of the members present vote in favor of it. But in no case shall the funds of the society be diverted from the purpose of promoting the cause of Peace, and abolishing the custom of

* Where the society is necessarily small, or where there is any difficulty in choosing proper officers ; the 4th article may be altered so as to constitute a committee of three or five, with power to fill vacancies or add to their number ; and the necessary verbal alterations made in the 3d and 6th articles.

War ; nor shall the amount of the subscriptions be increased without the consent of the subscribers.

NAMES.	SUMS SUBSCRIBED.

———

Peace Societies in the United States.

It is highly desirable that there should be more unanimity, intercourse and co-operation between the many peace societies established in this country than there have been. The great advantage of societies is that thereby the operations of individuals are directed to one and the same point, and so made efficient—as the rays of light are conveyed by a lens, and, (to learn from our opponents,) a whole battery of cannon is directed against one point, by which means a dark spot is illuminated, which would otherwise have remained in obscurity, and the stongest wall is prostrated, which would have been proof against ten times the number of cannon operating on different places and at different times. The same effect which is produced by an union of individuals is also produced by an union of societies, but on a larger scale. Now so far are the fifty peace societies of the United States from co-operation, that the names of the officers of the various societies are unknown to each other.

I can hardly let this subject pass, without endeavoring, still further, to impress on the mind of any friend of peace, who may chance to see this book, the absolute necessity of more union and co-operation among the friends of peace, than has yet appeared. A noble example has been set us by other benevolent institutions of our country. What but union has given force and power to the American Bible Society, the Foreign Missionary Society, the American Tract Society, Education Society, &c. ? It is obvious to the dullest observer, that, had there existed a number of independent, isolated bible societies, equal to the whole number now auxiliary to the great American Bible Society, very little effect would have been produced,—but, on the other hand, many of these small societies would have lingered out a short existence, and then sunk into obscurity and annihilation, and under the same circumstances, the same would have been the effect, with the other societies. *Union* gives strength— lessens the expense of publishing books and tracts favorable to the cause of peace, facilitates their circulation, and adds to the respectability and influence of a society. It is highly desirable, that a convention of delegates, from the various peace societies in the United States, should meet at some central place, such as New-York or Philadelphia, to consult on the best means of bringing about such an union, or at least of establishing some plan of co-operation.

Measures are now in operation for the formation of an American Peace Society, to embrace all the peace societies of North America; which desirable event is expected to take place within the present year.   Correspondence, (through the Rev. Noah Worcester, D. D., post-master, Brighton, Massachusetts,) on this, or any other subject, relating to the cause of peace, is solicited by

THE AUTHOR.

Feb. 1827.

ELEVENTH ANNUAL REPORT

OF THE

MASSACHUSETTS PEACE SOCIETY.

MORE than 700 years prior to the advent of the Messiah, the prophets, in foretelling the peaceful state of the world under his reign, made use of this language: "Nation shall not lift up sword against nation, neither shall they learn war any more." Such were to be the blessed effects of obedience to that gospel which proclaims peace on earth and good will to men. Eighteen centuries, however, have elapsed since the birth of our Saviour, and many nations have assumed the name of Christians. But, in respect to war, they have not distinguished themselves from Pagans and Mahometans, except it be by surpassing them in the duration of their conflicts, or in doing more to render the barbarous custom glorious and perpetual. Even since the close of the eighteenth century, all the nations of Christendom have been in arms, slaughtering one another, filling the earth with violence and wo, and glorying in their destructive enterprises.

Can it then be any longer wonderful, that many intelligent men have doubted the Divine authority of those predictions which relate to the reign of the Prince of Peace, and still ask, "Where is the promise of his coming?" And on what ground can Christians vindicate the pacific nature of their religion, against the sarcasms of unbelievers, but by appealing to the example and precepts of their Lord,—admitting that the wars of Christians have evinced a lamentable departure from the spirit of the gospel, and by showing that as soon as Christian nations shall act in character as the disciples of Christ, they will "learn war no more." To correct public opinion on this subject, by the diffusion of Christian sentiments, and thus to accelerate the accomplishment of prophecy, is the great object for which Peace Societies have been organized. The Committee have, therefore, deemed it proper in this Report to take a brief survey of the origin and progress of Peace Societies, and of some public occurrences favorable to their ultimate success.

The long and disastrous wars of Europe prior to 1815, in which our country became eventually involved, might naturally lead many Christians to reflect on the causes and effects of national hostilities, their contrariety to the spirit of the gospel,—and then to inquire whether something might not be done to open the eyes of men to their true interest, and thus to prevent the recurrence of such tornadoes of the human passions. From such reflections and inquiries probably originated the Peace Societies in this country and in Great Britain.

The first proposition for Peace Societies, known to the Committee, appeared in an anonymous Tract entitled, A Solemn Review of the Custom of War, which was offered for sale in Boston, on Christmas, December, 1814. As this work was written in time of war, and published at a period of remarkable party excitement, it might naturally give rise to suspicions in respect to its object. The Committee, however, are authorized to state, that the Tract did not originate from party spirit, nor from unfriendly feelings towards any class of people ; and that a particular object of the writer in causing it to be published at that critical period, was to prevent the horrors of civil war from being added to those of war with a foreign power. How early the first proposition for Peace Societies was made in England, the Committee are not able to state. But in July, 1815, a proposition of this kind was published in a periodical work, called "The Philanthropist." It was contained in a letter to the Editor, dated in April, which was probably earlier than the Solemn Review had been seen in that country.

In August 1815, the New York Peace Society was privately formed by a few respectable gentlemen, who deemed it prudent to keep the fact a secret for several months. On the second of December, the same year, the Ohio Peace Society was formed by some gentlemen who had read the Solemn Review, and who supposed their Society to be the first of the kind. On the 26th of the same month, the Constitution of the Massachusetts Peace Society was signed by twenty-two persons, the Rev. Dr. Osgood being the first subscriber. The Society for Promoting Permanent and Universal Peace was formed in London on the 14th of July, 1816. Thus four Peace Societies were formed in ten months, in regions far distant from each other.

It is not certainly known to the Committee how many Peace Societies have been formed in the United States; but the whole number reported of all descriptions, independent, auxiliary, and Reading Peace Societies, exceeds 50. It must however be acknowledged with regret, that several of these have discontinued their operations, if not their existence, and some others have done less than was expected of them.

The success of the London Peace Society has been annually increasing. At the time of its Tenth Annual Report, it had 49 auxiliaries, and a number of them both active and powerful. The distributions and sales of Tracts had in the preceding year amounted to 31,750, and the receipts of the Society in subscriptions and donations to more than 2400 dollars.

In Ireland a respectable Society is in operation, called the Hibernian Peace Society. In Nova Scotia and the Canadas several Peace Societies have been formed. In France, the Society of Christian Morals embraces several objects, one of which is the abolition of war ; and it is supposed this is the Society that was alluded to by a French nobleman at the last meeting of the British and Foreign Bible Society. As evidence of "improvement in public feeling" in France, he observed,—"I have assisted lately at the public meeting of a Society which has offered a prize for the best work on the causes of national hatred in general, and the means of extirpating it entirely." This work, if well written must give rise to discussions and inquiries which can hardly fail of a powerful and salutary influence, not only in France but in other countries.

For several years the operations of our Society have been unhappily restrained and limited by debt, which was incurred through delinquency in respect to the annual subscription. Wishing entirely to remove this embarrassment, the Committee have so limited the gratuitous distribution of tracts for the last year, that the whole of these, together with the sales, amount to no more than 10,-327. It is also to be remarked that a considerable part of this number of Tracts was distributed as the fruit of voluntary subscriptions from philanthropic individuals, who probably would not wish their names to be mentioned in this Report.

But notwithstanding all embarrassments, perhaps more has been done in the last year than in any that preceded, to advance the objects of the Society in our country. A number of newspapers have befriended the cause to a considerable extent. Four numbers of a work, called the Peace Observer, have been published in Buffalo, New-York, and distributed in different parts of the country. The valuable Essays on Peace and War by Philanthropos, which were originally published in the Christian Mirror at Portland, have been revised and published in a small volume, and nearly the whole edition has been sold or distributed.

Eleven new Societies have been formed,—one in each of the following places: Barre, Templeton, and Newburyport, in Massachusetts; Portsmouth and Exeter, in New-Hampshire; Buckfield, Brunswick, and Hebron, in Maine; Dorset in Vermont; Windham county in Connecticut; and one in Orange county, North Carolina. Six of these Societies were formed by the zeal and exertions of the gentleman who delivered our last anniversary address, and who has also been instrumental in reviving the Peace Society of Maine. His success evinces that much might be done in a short time, were there a competent number of energetic men devoted to the object.

The Committee would notice with approbation the Society recently formed in South Carolina, called the Anti-duelling Society. Its object is indicated by its name, and its exertions must render it an auxiliary to Peace Societies. All the arguments to prove that duelling is unnecessary and antichristian, or that a method not murderous may be adopted for settling the disputes of individuals, can be easily applied to the quarrels of governments. And as the wars of nations are far more demoralizing, calamitous, and unjust in their operations, than the wars of duellists, those who now perceive that duelling is detestable and barbarous, and that exertions ought to be made to abolish the custom, are in a fair way to discover that still greater exertions should be made to render public war disreputable, and to effect its abolition. In both cases the smiles of Heaven may be expected to accompany benevolent exertions ; and when public opinion shall have been duly enlightened, both customs will be found as unnecessary, as they are calamitous and antichristian.

As an auspicious event, the Committee had occasion to notice in their Tenth Report, the adjustment of differences between Great Britain and the United States by a friendly reference to the emperor Alexander. Since that period a serious difficulty between Portugal and Brazil has been settled by the mediation of George IV. These events clearly show that the principles of Christianity and civilization are as applicable to the disputes of nations, as to the contentions of individuals. They also evince a growing disposition on the part of governments to adopt these principles in preference to the barbarous tribunal of the sword.

Our own government has also displayed the spirit of philanthropy in employing its influence and agency to prevent hostilities be-

tween the various tribes of Indians ; and also
in its efforts to obtain treaties for the abolition of the piratical practice of privateering
in time of war.   In a Message of the President to the House of Representatives, during
the last session of Congress, on the Panama
Mission, he gave evidence that the abolition
of privateering was an object near to his heart.
This may appear from the following im-
pressive passage.—" If it be true that the no-
blest treaty of peace ever mentioned in history, is that by which the Carthaginians were
bound to abolish the practice of sacrificing
their own children, *because it was stipulated in
favor of human nature*, I cannot exaggerate to
myself the unfading glory with which these
United States will go forth in the memory of
future ages, if by friendly counsel, by their
moral influence, by the power of argument
and persuasion alone, they can prevail on the
American nations at Panama to stipulate by
general agreement among themselves, and so
far as any of them may be concerned, the
perpetual abolition of private war on the
ocean."

  Should this object be attained, and acceded
to by the other maritime powers, it will be
the most important step that ever was taken
by the governments of Christendom.   It will
greatly diminish the motives to war, and of
course its frequency.   Besides, it will constitute an eminence, from which may be seen
the total abolition of public war.   For the inquiry will immediately arise,—if governments,

by a friendly compact, can dispense with privateering, why not with every species of war on the ocean, and on the land?

It is also worthy of remark, that the President of the Congress of Panama, in his introductory speech, considered the prevention of future wars, by an improved code of international law, as a particular object of their meeting; and having mentioned what had heretofore been proposed and written in favor of settling national controversies by arbitration, he says,—" Let us avoid war by a common and uniform reference to negotiation."

As further proof that God is preparing the way to bless the world with peace, it may be proper to mention the remarkable change which has occurred among the inhabitants of the Society Islands. In former years their wars were not only frequent, but of the most terrible and exterminating character. But now " their wars are at an end. The weapons of war are neglected and are perishing." This has been certified by a respectable English missionary, who spent several years among that people, and who has since visited our country. This remarkable change in the character of the people was the effect of their receiving the gospel of peace as the word of the living God. And the inhabitants of the Sandwich Islands seem to be in a fair way to follow this noble example. But how melancholy is the fact that the English and American missionaries were not able to assure these islanders, that the gospel had produced similar effects in their respective countries ! On the contrary, if they have been full and explicit on the subject, they must have confessed the humiliating fact, that although the gospel so clearly requires of all Christians the meek and forbearing spirit of Jesus their Lord, yet perhaps there are no Pagan countries on earth in which the spirit and deeds of war are more celebrated than in Great Britain and the United States, or where people are at so much expense to keep alive the spirit of war, and to teach manslaughter as a science both necessary and honorable !

Hitherto the progress of light and truth has been slow ; but the laudable spirit of improvement in regard to the means and modes of education which is now prevalent, affords reason to hope that the future progress of light will be far more rapid than the past. The improvements already made, will naturally lead to improvements still greater. In several countries efforts are now making to extend the blessings of education to the young of both sexes, and of every class. If due care shall also be taken to imbue the youthful mind with Christian sentiments, or to give to the means of improvement a truly moral and religious direction, the time may soon arrive, when it will be found far more easy to *prevent war* than to *find soldiers* for that inhuman employment. For an aversion to war will be the natural effect of training up children in the way they should go. Unchris·

tian education, in time past, rendered wars inevitable. Christian education, in time to come, may render wars impossible, or confine them to freebooters and bucaniers.

That all Christians should be friends of peace ;—that all Christian rulers, and all ministers of the gospel should be peace makers,—and that all Christian churches should be Peace Societies, are truths as evident to the enlightened mind, as that the example of our Lord is worthy to be imitated, or his precepts worthy to be obeyed, or his gospel worthy of all acceptation. No other thing, it is presumed, has done so much to prevent the progress of the gospel among Jews, Pagans, and Mahometans, or to multiply Deists in Christian lands, or to retard the fulfilment of prophecy respecting the peace of the world, as the inconsistency of professed Christians in giving celebrity to the principles and enterprises of war. If, then, the promised success of the gospel, and the accomplishment of the most glorious predictions, are objects of importance ; so important it is, that Christians of all denominations should unite their efforts to disseminate and impress the principles of peace, and to render war the abhorrence of man.

Note.—Since the above was published, a large peace society has been instituted at Andover, Mass., embracing the professors of the theological institution, most of the students, and many of the inhabitants of the town ; and similar societies are anticipated, in all our theological seminaries.

15*

INDEX.